COME OUT AND BE SEPARATE!

Rick S. Bell

"Therefore, come out from among them and be ye separate," saith the Lord.

2Corinthians 6:17

Come Out and Be Separate!

ISBN-13: 978-1466486805
ISBN-10: 1466486805
Copyright © 2000, 2011 by Rick S. Bell

All rights reserved. No part of this book may be reproduced or transmitted in any form or by any means without written permission of the author.

Unless otherwise noted, Scripture taken from the King James Version.

Visit www.ricksbell.com

Contents

Introduction 1

1. Who Needs to Come Out? 5

2. Why We Must Come Out 15

3. How to Come Out and Be Separate 23

4. Coming Out in Fellowship 29

5. Coming Out with Joy 37

6. Coming Out to Serve 43

7. Coming Out of a Rut 49

8. One Place NOT to Come Out Of 57

9. Into the Wilderness 63

10. The Results of Coming Out 71

Study Guide 77

Preface

This book is both old and new. I first published *Come Out and Be Separate* in the year 2000. At that time, I was influenced greatly by the kind of writing that challenges and critiques everything that is wrong within the church. I developed a critical eye and vented out my judgment upon the printed pages. I tried to write as a prophet, and I thought I was tempering everything with at least some kindness and grace. Little did I realize just how legalistic I really was.

In recent years, I experienced a spiritual revolution in my life. I discovered just how amazing grace is! I had a complete paradigm shift, and realized that I had previously been under a subtle system of law and works. I believed in grace and the forgiveness of sins, yet felt that God was always angry with me when I messed up. I based my relationship with Him on how well I was doing, more than on the truth of His unconditional love and the finished work of Christ on the cross.

I went back and looked at some of the old books I had written. They now appeared too critical and Puritan-sounding. They acknowledged grace but there was too much guilt motivation. *Come Out* was among them! To make matters worse, I had given hundreds of copies away when we went to speak at churches while on furlough.

Nonetheless, some people still liked the book. Though written from a wrong perspective, there were still good and important things worth considering. After my paradigm shift, I believed the Lord wanted me to go back and fix things. I re-did my first book, *Win Christ*, and the response was overwhelmingly positive. Next in line for surgery was *Come Out and Be Separate*. What you hold in your hands now is the third re-write.

This is a book about holiness, written from a grace perspective. Most of the time holiness is addressed in a legalistic way or it is not addressed at all. This is an attempt to encouraging holy living by presenting it as desirable and without condemnation.

Lots of the original work was cut from this edition. A Bible Study was added. There was a complete overhaul on language and tone. There are a few sections that I considered cutting altogether, but ended up leaving them in because they made important points. I didn't want to be afraid to mention hard things, but I wanted to mention them softly!

The end result, I believe, is an easy to read and uplifting book. I hope it blesses and encourages you.

Rick Bell
China, 2011

Introduction

MANY YEARS AGO, two young men decided to add a little adventure into their lives. During a lunch break from work, one suggested to the other, "Let's go skydiving!"

"That sounds great!" said the other, figuring they would never *really* go through with it. But after weeks of talking, they found themselves on their way to an airfield just outside the city.

Chatting nervously in the car, the two chuckled as they considered that what they were about to do was absolutely crazy! Upon their arrival, they were greeted with a stack of forms to sign. The first one was a waiver of responsibility for the skydiving company. It did little to alleviate their fears, stating in very large letters:

"WARNING: SKYDIVING IS A SPORT THAT CAN RESULT IN SERIOUS INJURIES AND EVEN DEATH."

After signing the waiver and paying their fees, the two were led into a classroom to begin a six-hour orientation before actually going up in the plane. They watched a video that described various situations that could go wrong. The video ended with a greeting from the president of the company who also said, "Remember, this is a sport that can result in death. You are here by your own choice!" Then, for the next half of the day, they were taught what to watch out for and what to do in case of possible parachuting problems.

That day was filled with just about every emotion imaginable. At times the two would sweat with fear, and other times they would fill with excitement. When it started to rain, they were stricken with threats of disappointment. In the end, however, the weather let up and the two were eventually airborne!

The first one dropped off the plane, pulled his cord, and out popped the parachute. There was only one small problem—it didn't open! The procedure was to count to seven and the chute should open. But as he counted to TEN he saw his life flashing before his eyes! Then he remembered his emergency cord, and just as he reached for it, the chute finally unfurled. Better late than never!

The other young man dropped off the plane and had no problems at all. Through a radio, he listened to instructions from a professional on the ground. The pro helped him steer correctly to the base. He was puzzled, though, when his guide told him to "flare the chute" in preparation for landing. It seemed too early! But he did so, and a second or two later he was safely on the ground.

He had made the mistake of looking down, and his perception was off (the ground was closer than it appeared). His timing was off because he paid no attention to the horizon. If he had failed to flare the chute when he was told, he would have hit the ground too hard and probably broken some bones.

Like skydiving, the Christian life can be a thrilling experience. But only the daring will come to understand this. Not everyone wants **to come out from among them and be…separate (2 Cor.6:17).** And there are some who go up in the plane but never make the necessary leap of faith. There are others who do but their perception is off, and they miss the beauty of the horizon. Others fall with their parachutes unopened, unprepared for the trials that come, because they never gave themselves to the proper orientation.

As we enter into these "last of the last days," it is crucial that the church comes out of the closets of institutionalism, formalism and surface religion. It is time to glow in the realms of grace, faith and love. The darkness is increasing in the land, so the calling to shine is urgent. As with skydiving, there are many dangers around us. The last thing we want is to be found with a faith that never unfurled!

Reorientation

In his philosophical treatise, *Nature,* Ralph Waldo Emerson wrote:

> To speak truly, few adult persons can see nature. Most persons do not see the sun. At least they have a very superficial seeing. The sun illuminates only the eye of the man, but shines into the eye and the heart of the child.

Though I wouldn't agree with the total of his essay, this excerpt is instructive. Emerson tries to reorient the common person's understanding of nature. He wants us to see past the ordinary and be transformed by the sublime. The same must be done in the Christian life. We already know something about faith, hope, and love, but we need to become like children—seeing past our walls of doctrine and prejudicial haze. We need to clear our 'spiritual sinuses' and breathe in the life that pulses within these heavenly principles. It is not just knowing *about* these things, but being enlivened by them. We don't want it to be said of the church, "truly, few adult persons can see."

* * * * *

I write this little book to you from the far away land of China. In China, you must learn how to use chopsticks if you do not want to go hungry. At first it is very awkward as your fingers try to adjust to the strange new way of getting food into your mouth. Later, however, it becomes quite natural, and in some cases easier to use than a fork. This is also how it is with reorientation. I invite every reader to come to this with a mind to put down the fork of their common understanding and take up the chopsticks of faith—for true Christians should reckon themselves foreigners in any land, as **they desire a better country, that is a heavenly one (Heb.11:16; NASB).**

In China, I am immediately recognized as a foreigner. I am immediately perceived as being different. The need of the day is for a dying world to perceive Christians as foreigners in this earthly realm. That is what we are! And it is still possible to come out and stand out as **a chosen generation, a royal priesthood, a holy nation, a peculiar people, that [we] shew forth the praises of Him who hath called [us] out of darkness into His marvelous light (1Pet.2:9).**

What does it mean to come out and be separate, and how might this actually be done? These are the questions that are considered here. I believe that the reader who perseveres through this short book will find encouragement along the way. To "come out and be separate" is to embark on a most rewarding journey. Why stay in and miss out?

1. Who Needs to Come Out?

HAVE YOU EVER gone searching through your closet and found something that you completely forgot about? Sometimes we can actually forget about valuables and never get to enjoy them while they just sit useless in the dark. Now all true Christians possess the most wonderful riches and are capable of shining the brightest light. We remain in the dark, however, when we neglect to bring these valuables out.

Consider your riches: There are billionaires that have nothing compared to you, IF you have yielded your life to Jesus Christ and received Him as your Lord and Savior. If you have laid down your life to live for Him, you have a greater inheritance than anyone else in this world can claim! You have been blessed **with all spiritual blessings in heavenly places in Christ (Eph.1:3).** One taste of this is worth more than all the treasuries the world can produce. Even if your wallets are thin, you can be classified with the apostle Paul as **having nothing and yet possessing all things (2 Cor. 6:10).**

But notice the word I used: *taste.* It will not suffice to just understand this precious truth. It must be tasted. **O TASTE and see that the LORD is good (Ps.34:8).** This means that the truth becomes more than just an idea or concept. It is experienced in such a way that it satisfies your life's hunger and causes a desire for more.

The spiritual tasting of truth is a sure way to bring out our riches and shine for the world. Jesus instructed, **"You are the light of the world. A city on a hill cannot be hidden. Neither do people light a lamp and put it under a bowl. Instead they put it on its stand, and it gives light to everyone in the house" (Matt.5:14-15; NIV).** It is necessary to come out from under the bowl and show this dark world the beams that shine from heaven.

Easier Said than Done

In the land of China there are many Christian workers from other countries. One of their greatest challenges is that they cannot be overtly involved as 'ministers of the gospel' or 'evangelists'. The communist country will not permit visas for such, and will deport those caught doing overt evangelical activity.

The missionaries must live as 'normal' citizens, either to work or to study in a secular setting (although there are a few exceptions). In order to reach the lost, they must depend on the Lord to move in great ways through relationships and the right opportunities to share the good news. This often takes time, and since they (by necessity) spend a lot of time in secular activity, it is easy to grow spiritually weary and desire to move on. If they were caught up in the fervor of evangelical crusades and open-air ministry they might be encouraged daily by the very nature of their work. It would feel more like they were serving the Lord. Instead, they often have to wait, and wait, and wait. Many do not feel like missionaries when they have to witness mostly by simply living.

There are other difficulties, as well. I have visited several villages in the Chinese countryside. The tribal people groups usually speak a different language from the standard Chinese. In fact, there are so many languages among the different peoples and localities that in one village I thought, "even if we were allowed to preach here, we couldn't do it!" There I was at the ends of the earth feeling helpless as a baby. As far as the Great Commission was concerned, we were so close, and yet so far!

Those who work in modern day China can sometimes feel like closet Christians. They cannot "shout it from the rooftops." But there are other ways they can 'come out.' Their mission activity must involve the encouraging of their own faith, that they might be ready to see God move in their helpless situations. He can move in China, He has moved, and He will yet move! At times we might feel helpless as a baby, but we can't be babies about it. We have to come out in faith, hope, and love, and then He will come out and overcome the odds.

Years later, I was able to bring some tribal Christians from Thailand into the very villages where I had felt so helpless. They were of the same people group, and they could speak the language! The gospel was preached and heard. It was so exciting to see God moving in ways that I had never dreamed of earlier.

Where do you work, or where do you go to school? Are the odds against you? Most likely, yes. But if you have a willing heart, God will make a way. Be faithful and remember to be patient. He is working even when we do not perceive it.

One's immediate understanding of a situation may bring the temptation to feel frustration or despair, but there is a way out: **Trust in the LORD with all your heart and lean not on your own understanding (Prov.3:5)**. This is a lesson that needs to be learned over and over again, because it is so easy to look at the externals and take our cues from them. The born again Christian is a supernatural creation, and must learn to take his or her cues from the promises of God, even when all else seems to be suggesting otherwise. **In all thy ways acknowledge Him, and He shall direct thy paths (Prov.3:6)**. It may take some time for the paths to straighten out, but there can be peace right now in the simple acknowledging that He is there and that He is working.

He must be acknowledged when things are going smoothly, as well. The danger for a lot of Christians is that they can get caught up in religious works without truly acknowledging Jesus. Their Christian separation can be more Pharisaical than devotional. In serving the Lord, it is necessary to take care that we focus more on WHO we serve rather than on what we actually do.

The Fruit is Left in the Bowl

It does not take a great Christian to be involved in overt Christian activity. In fact, it can be easier to be *deceived* in such settings. How many people throughout America would say they are Christians because they go to church every week? And yet there are many who do not know Jesus. How many sad stories are there of pastors and missionaries who have fallen into sin? They were involved in 'great works' but they lost track of their own hearts.

Proverbs 4:23 exhorts, **"Keep thy heart with all diligence, for out of it are the issues of life."** Someone wisely said, "Many know much, but few know themselves." God's love is unconditional, but it is good to check and see whether we are operating from His springs of eternal life, or if there are polluted waters that first need to be flushed out of the way.

I knew of a man who continually spoke of the Lord with apparent love and desire. He wanted to go into mission work and he met with others for this purpose. He loved to sing and lead in worship. But when his friends discovered some of his unethical activities, they confronted him. He became as a spider, disregarding their concerns and continuing to weave his unsavory web! Even in his obvious manipulations, he did not stop with his religious rhetoric.

I knew of a woman who seemed to be very susceptible to the moves of the Holy Spirit. She often fell to the floor in worship. Yet her sister confessed hearing her frequently lose her temper and yelling at other people when she wasn't at church.

Other Christians have pushed and shoved and demanded their rights, fighting tooth and nail rather than heeding Paul's advice, **"Why not rather be wronged?" (1Cor.6:7; NIV).** The Lord will vindicate! Are vengeful Christians spiritual people? Maybe. But if so, something is wrong. A.B. Simpson revealed great insight when he wrote:

> The heart in which the Holy Spirit lives will always be characterized by gentleness, lowliness, quietness, meekness and forbearance. The rude, sarcastic spirit, the brusque manner, the sharp retort, the unkind cut-- all these belong to the flesh.[1]

---

[1] Simpson, A.B., *The Holy Spirit*, p.7.

I don't judge these people mentioned above, but add myself to the list! There was a time in China when my family moved to another city. Our old landlord, a kind old Chinese man, informed us that we owed him some money after we had already moved. We were perplexed. We thought we had paid him all that was necessary. When he explained it over the phone it was unclear. It had something to do with outstanding bills, which we thought were all covered. We told him we would call him when we returned for a visit to his city the next month.

It was not uncommon for some Chinese to try and take advantage of us 'foreigners.' All the while I kept thinking, "Why is he cheating us? I didn't think *he* would take advantage of us! It's not fair!" When we came up the next month we stayed at a hotel. My wife said, "How are we going to get to him?"

"Get to him?" I snarled. "He should come to us. He will be getting his money. Let him come to the hotel." A perfectly justifiable attitude, right?

It turned out when he came, the bills were not as much as we had thought, and they were indeed legitimate. He was sweet and kind, and he even brought our child a little gift. We paid him and he offered to house us whenever we came to his city for a visit. We said goodbye, and he would get back on a bus to go across the city. How terrible I felt after that!

The dear sweet man was not trying to cheat us. The Holy Spirit convicted me that *even if the man was cheating,* the true Christ-like thing to do was to go to him. The true Christ-like thing is to **bless them that curse you, do good to them that hate you (Matt.5:44).**

We should also **give preference to one another in honor (Rom.12:10; NASB).** Early on in my spiritual journey I attended an Urbana Missions conference. The meetings were held in the university's coliseum. At night the buses would come and take all the attendees back to their dorms. It happened to be the coldest time of the year. When the meetings were over each night, the freezing students would bob up and down outside waiting for the buses. When the buses finally came, it was stampede time! Sheer madness ensued as everyone raced to get on before everybody else. Few people waited behind to endure the cold, in preference to their brothers and sisters.

"But it was cold!" I hear one argue. Exactly. That was the cross that no one wanted to bear.

A brother told me that when he worked as a waiter, he dreaded most waiting on church groups. He said that they often "order you around and want things just perfect or they complain and ask for more. Then they leave a minuscule tip, or worse, just a tract!" Not all groups are like this, but when this happens it presents a terrible witness on two accounts: it shows the inflexibility of those who should be humble and considerate, and the stinginess of those who should be generous.

These examples touch the heart of Christian living and witness. Not going to conferences, not being involved in works, or hanging inspirational plaques on the wall, but being filled with the Spirit and living as Christ.

I'm not saying this to condemn anybody, but to get us thinking in terms of the Kingdom. God loves us and forgives us. We all fall short, and there is no condemnation in Jesus! Yet the call is to come out and be separate. To come out is to enjoy the fresher air, and we all need more of this to some degree or another. The goal of Christian living is to be able to say, **"I live, yet not I, but Christ liveth in me" (Galatians 2:20).**

It is an awesome life if the life of God is in you. But it has to be Him, and not us trying to imitate or act like Him. He needs to be received by faith. He has promised His Holy Spirit to those who ask. If you have not received or been filled with the Holy Spirit, you can ask for Him to enter in and He will (**Luke 11:13**)!

Certainly many would confess that they want to live quality Christian lives. But it is not enough just to confess it. It requires faith and a commitment to the Lord's Kingdom principles. It is our privilege to come out—to take steps of faith and bring out the amazing grace that the Lord has placed inside each one of us.

In even the most nominal believer- if there is any true work of grace in the heart- there is the hope of glory. It seems that many Christians do not believe or give much thought to **the hope of glory** that is in them (**Col. 1:27**). They care more for the externals: the meetings, the rituals, the appearances, the works, the excitements, and so on. **Christ in you** awaits to come out and truly be manifested. It takes a humble attitude, trust, and faith that He is working. Then walk accordingly.

It's All About Love

It is all too easy to work up a FORM of righteousness, morals, and even spiritual knowledge. The ways of Jesus, however, work through love from the inside out. That means loving Him above all else, which means loving self less. This won't happen, though, unless you first believe and receive the love that He has for you. **We love Him because He first loved us (1John 4:19).**

Do you picture God as always angry with you, only tolerating you from afar? Then it won't work. That is not believing in Him with gospel faith in Jesus Christ. Gospel faith is believing what is written in **Romans 5:8-11:**

> **But God commendeth his love toward us, in that, while we were yet sinners, Christ died for us.**
> **Much more then, being now justified by his blood, we shall be saved from wrath through him.**
> **For if, when we were enemies, we were reconciled to God by the death of his Son, much more, being reconciled, we shall be saved by his life.**
> **And not only so, but we also joy in God through our Lord Jesus Christ, by whom we have now received the atonement.**

See yourself no longer as an enemy, and do not be so proud as to think you cannot receive the life and forgiveness that God wants to give. Then sweeten the pot and believe the words of **Isaiah 54:8-10** as if they were spoken directly to you:

> **In a little wrath I hid my face from thee for a moment; but with everlasting kindness will I have mercy on thee, saith the LORD thy Redeemer.**

> **For this is as the waters of Noah unto me: for as I have sworn that the waters of Noah should no more go over the earth; so have I sworn that I would not be angry with thee, nor rebuke thee.**
> **For the mountains shall depart, and the hills be removed; but my kindness shall not depart from thee, neither shall the covenant of my peace be removed, saith the LORD that hath mercy on thee.**
> **(Isa 54:8-10)**

Remember the words of Jesus: **"It is finished" (John 19:30).** None of your works or lack of works is going to undo what He has done. He has satisfied the requirements of the law for you. Your failures are not going to re-institute the law against you. It's over! **And through Him everyone who believes is freed from all things, from which you could not be freed through the Law of Moses (Acts 13:39; NASB).**

Every believer's work of faith is to **keep [themselves] in the love of God (Jude 21).** So many lose sight of the love and fall prey to the subtle idea of working to please God, ultimately going back to the law. It is faith that pleases God, and He wants us to abide in His *love*, not law (**1John 4:16**).

When believers really understand that God gave Himself for them in love, it will cause them to want to give themselves back to Him as well. Most people place self first and want more, more, more. It just doesn't seem to compute that laying down personal agendas would be the best thing one could do. Yet Jesus had it all and left glory to suffer shame and humiliation, even death on a cross! He suffered everything for us. It didn't seem to compute when He was nailed to that cross in Israel. Yet because of this, **God also hath highly exalted Him, and given Him a name which is above every name (Phil.2:9).** If we would come out and be separate, the desire will be to follow Him, come what may. But it is much easier to stay in and want more, more, more. It is easier to give in to the flesh rather than give way for the Spirit. But a revelation of His love is all it takes to motivate us.

Following Jesus requires courage. However, it need not be fearful, because His yoke is easy and His burden is light. The steps ahead may at times seem difficult, but if we step up in faith, He will meet us in the air. He will come and lead us into higher realms. We will find that it is the most fragrant air, and our communion with Him will be exhilarating. There will be strength for every step of the way, and before long we will wonder why we ever waited so long to come out in the first place!

2. Why We Must Come Out

> **For ye are the temple of the living God; as God hath said, I will dwell in them, and walk in them; and I will be their God, and they shall be my people.**
> **Wherefore come out from among them, and be ye separate, saith the Lord, and touch not the unclean thing; and I will receive you,**
> **And will be a Father unto you, and ye shall be my sons and daughters, saith the Lord Almighty.**
> **(2Corinthians 6:16-18)**

I'M TEMPTED to let this chapter end here. The Scripture quoted above gives reason enough why we should come out. This passage contains a wonderful promise- the great and glorious God will even be our own God, as a father to His sons and daughters. He will dwell in us and walk among us; and the very life of Christ will be our victory. We shoot ourselves in the foot when we stay in the mainstream. We may be able to live a successful 'religious' life, but there is a special and divine joy that only comes to those who become separate. The consecrated Christian finds communion, power, and peace from God. He can walk on the waters of this life abiding in his Savior.

If somebody walks on the water, as Jesus and Peter did, they are sure to get noticed. It is the supernatural in the life of a Christian that will truly witness to the world. The world has seen plenty of religious meetings and traditions. It has heard good religious teaching and exciting Christian rhetoric. But the world does not quite know what to think when they see a Christian loving his or her enemies. It takes notice when a Christian shows patience in the most trying circumstances. If it sees a joyful Christian in the midst of suffering, it marvels. It cannot argue with miracles. None of these can be accomplished without the supernatural working of God in our lives. On the other hand, it does not require supernatural working to buy religious books, go to church, or criticize others' theology on the internet.

True Separation

An American co-worker in China brought us some exciting news from home:

"My dad has been saved!"

We rejoiced to hear that another soul had entered the family of God. Full of excitement, the worker told a Chinese believer, "My dad has become a Christian!"

She replied, "What? I thought all Americans were Christian."

Well, it is true that America was founded on Christian principles and has been thought of as a 'Christian nation.' Today it would be better described as 'Post-Christian.' The problem was that the Chinese friend's perception was off. The communist party equates Christianity with democracy and capitalism. It is blinded to the very essence of the Christian faith, which is a matter of life and truth.

Before we get too hard on our misguided friends, though, consider the American perception. It has already been observed that many equate the Christian faith with traditions and works. This deception can be traced back all the way to Cain (Gen.4), who based his religion on what he offered. We see it exemplified in the Pharisees and Sadducees, who **strain at a gnat and swallow a camel (Matt.23:24).** They tithe **mint and anise and cummin, and have omitted the weightier matters of the law: judgment, mercy, and faith (vs.23).**

America is the land of busyness. Everybody is coming and going, doing and doing. Some like to boast, "I'm so busy. I have little time!" Ministries are not devoid of this. If someone is not deceived by a religion of self-righteousness, they may be deceived by a religion of works. The

Protestants accuse the Catholics of this, but it is very much alive throughout the evangelical church. It's just more sneaky and subtle. We can pride ourselves on sound doctrine and love for the Word, and all the while be caught up in a whirlwind of works to satisfy our consciences. Many get so busy maintaining the camp, when they need to go outside of the camp and meet with Jesus (**Heb.13:13**). Our main work is to enter into His REST. We are justified by faith!

Another American perception of the Christian faith is caught up in what I call "the flower market of religion." This is the cash register of Christianity. We have trinkets, T-shirts, music, books, and videos. We now have a specially-themed Bible for every interest. We have bumper stickers and bracelets, greeting cards and computer games. In themselves and in their proper places, there may not be anything wrong with these. The problem though, is that we have become inundated with them. It is quite possible to 'learn the lingo,' immerse oneself into the 'Christian subculture' and mistake that for being a person of faith. But this is not the same as coming out and being separate in the Biblical sense.

"I'm so discouraged, my best friend is living with a guy," complains a young woman. "This guy isn't treating her well, and she still refuses to leave. And the worst thing about it is that they're both believers!" If they really are believers, it seems they are not living out what they believe, or they believe the wrong things. The Christian community sometimes encourages believers like this by presenting faulty perceptions of what Biblical faith is. Let me explain.

Biblical separation means living differently. It does not mean snubbing the world, but it does mean being clearly distinct from the world. And how is a Christian clearly distinct from the world? The answer is in *holiness*. The very word holiness means *not common*, or *set apart*. The problem today is that the church often preaches holy living in a legalistic context, or it rarely mentions holiness at all. Without thumping people with Bibles, and with a clear understanding of its benefits, we should spur one another on to a much higher standard than that of the world. The message coming from the Christian subculture, however, often implies that conformity is okay. Here are some examples:

• An evangelical pastor lamented from the pulpit the end of a successful running sitcom on television. The sitcom was known for its dirty jokes and irreverence. The pastor's endorsement suggests that there's no problem with watching the show. "If Pastor watches it, it must be okay!"

Watching a show like that won't send you to hell, and there may even be some good things in it, in spite of the bad. We have grace and are free to watch whatever we want. But if we want to go far spiritually, we will need to guard our hearts and minds from the sinful influence that is pervasive in the media. A continual exposure to dirty language and innuendos makes it more difficult to resist wrong thoughts and other temptations that come.

• Sadly, many Christians have become ensnared in pornography. It is now spoken as simply a given: "most men are going to struggle with this sin." Without denying that it is a huge problem, the church should not accept it as "a given." If it is going to be addressed, it should not be considered as a 'normal' vice that Christians fall into. It should be considered shocking, no matter how widespread the epidemic has become. We are more ready to fight a temptation we see as shocking than one seen as normal.

Have you fallen into this? You already know that it is a fire that brings misery in the end. But it is no match for Jesus! He loves us in spite of the filth we've been in, and He can easily deliver us. Say no to the sin, and give Him a chance. If you slip again, believe the truth that there is no condemnation in Christ. That is the good news of the gospel! That sin has been paid for and God is not angry with you. Thank Him and worship Him for that, then say no again to the sin. If you fail again, start over again—thanking God for His forgiveness and love. As many times as it takes.

• A celebrity, after recently having an affair, was back in the spotlight on Christian television, and the forgiving host of the show gleefully scorned any critics, saying, "As if they've never made a mistake!" We do need to be forgiving, but an affair is more than a mistake. It can bring much pain and grief to many lives.

We need less critics and we don't have to be judgmental, but let's not gloss over serious transgressions with light dismissals. This is not about condemning others, but encouraging them to stay on the right course. Sometimes it is necessary to shout, "Danger ahead!"

- Many contemporary Christian musicians don the current fashions and trends of the world. This is not necessarily wrong, but sometimes it goes too far.

Once on furlough, I attended a secular teacher's conference that happened to be held at a local seminary. A poster at the seminary touted an upcoming concert by a Christian rock group. They didn't have to look like angels. They didn't have to look like the clean-cut gospel quartets that Grandma Sally used to listen to. But this group looked like a bunch of angry gang members. I'm sure they were just trying to appeal to a frustrated youth market. But I thought about how some of the non-believers at the conference might have seen the ad. Jesus came to bring life abundantly, and we represent the King! The message this group was sending was: be angry and sour.

- A famous Christian commentator frequently recommended films, in spite of questionable content. Alfred Hitchcock's films were once recommended for the purpose of 'sharing with others' the clearly defined differences between good and evil. He said that it was Hitchcock's 'religious upbringing' that gave him such an ability to understand and portray the differences vividly in his films.

If you get a thrill from exposing yourself to evil, so be it. But it is better to be **simple concerning evil (Rom.16:19).** That means not yielding to things which are wrong. When we expose ourselves to unholy elements (like violent horror films), we make it harder on ourselves to grow spiritually and to walk in victory. Satan can use those images to disturb us later. It can become more difficult to sense the presence of the Lord's love. Why recommend things that have the potential to harden our hearts?

Remember that the root word of 'Protestant' is protest. The church's job is to protest against sin and evil, apathy, irreverence, and the norm. But I am NOT suggesting we start blasting everyone around us and crushing everybody in righteous indignation. That would clearly be wrong! Yet people often go to the other extreme and never make a stand for anything, because they do not want to appear prudish.

The last thing we want is to be modern day Pharisees, but it is possible to protest in love. The way of the Lord is the way of love. It is possible to humbly pursue righteousness. We can view ourselves as more *in the* world but not *of the* world. This doesn't mean sticking our noses up at everyone. It means keeping a prayerful watch over our hearts while we love others but stay separate from any ungodly values. Separation from those values, while showing love and care to those who hold them, is an effective way to do it. It may even cause others to follow our example.

Now or Later

We have a choice. We can continue on in faulty perceptions and tread the path of mediocrity, or we can decide to "touch no unclean thing" and learn the powerful paths of true life in Christ. We can either stay with the children on the playground or we can suit up in holy armor and become more than conquerors.

Finally, **examine yourselves, whether ye be in the faith; prove your own selves (2 Cor.13:5).** This doesn't just mean, "make sure you are saved." It means give some thought to what you are producing. Are you living out your faith or is it just a set of teachings you happen to agree with? The Christian faith is a precious faith, **more precious than gold (1 Pet. 1:7).** Yet some carry their faith like a child playing with an expensive vase. They don't know what they've truly got and they get close to fumbling it to their loss.

The better way is to **walk worthy of the God who hath called you unto His kingdom and glory (1 Thess. 2:12).** When we start living according to His ways, we become more in tune with the divine. We find more strength for the battles ahead. We enjoy the blessings of His kingdom, which remains unshaken while everything else is falling apart. He has entrusted us with riches beyond what we can immediately perceive. A life's pursuit of walking worthy will bring these out in due time. He will bless a pursuit like this, and we can trust Him to bring it to success.

This is why we should come out and be separate: it's good for us, and it brings glory to God. It's good for us in that we get out of the faulty perceptions that drag us down and keep us from experiencing God's best.

God's best is for now, not just the age to come. It brings glory to God when we walk in His best, and we represent Him in truth while working through a world so full of destructive lies.

3. How to Come Out and Be Separate

REMEMBER THE STORY OF THE PRODIGAL?

> **For she said, 'I will go after my lovers,**
> **that give me my bread and my water,**
> **my wool and my flax, mine oil and my drink.'**
> **Therefore, behold, I will hedge up thy way**
> **with thorns, and make a wall, that she shall**
> **not find her paths.**
> **And she shall follow after her lovers, but she**
> **shall not overtake them; And she shall seek**
> **them, but shall not find them. Then shall**
> **she say, 'I will go and return to my first husband,**
> **for then was it better for me than now.'**
> **(Hosea 2:5-7).**

Perhaps you were expecting the more familiar passage about the wayward son who left the pigs to return to his father (**Luke 15**)? Both give an excellent example of turning away from the world and being restored to the divine. The prodigal son learns of the wonderful love of his Father. The prodigal wife is brought back to her senses.

The wife in this passage represents Israel, but we may apply it to ourselves spiritually. This text, like the more familiar prodigal son text, does not illustrate a conversion experience. The main characters already belong to the Lord. However, they are not aligned with Him but with the ways of the world. They both find carnal thrills and joy in the most sinful of situations, until they hit bottom and realize the ugliness of it all.

The prodigal son is treated to more than he ever expected: mercy, forgiveness and celebration. Israel also will be treated to a most divine gift, the intimate love of the Lord as their Husband:

> "In that day," declares the LORD, "you will call me 'my husband'; you will no longer call me 'my master.'" (Hosea 2:16; NIV).

What a thrilling prospect! The law-oriented traditional religion of Judaism will give way to an intimate bonding with God, as a Husband relates to a wife.

It is a lesson for the church. When we, like the prodigal wife, come to our senses and separate ourselves from the grasps of the world, we will experience a great change in our relationship with God. So many fail to experience the sweet manifestations of God's love because they are still dabbling in worldly husks and know Him only as 'Master.' The first step necessary for coming out of this is to see the present surroundings for what they are. We need to come to our spiritual senses.

Not Without a Vision

You may be thinking, "I'm not seeking other lovers, I'm not in the pigpen. This is old news!" It may be old news, but do not forget that the prodigals were blinded for a season. For a season they thought nothing was wrong. We in the church should know better when we are in the midst of terrible sin; however, it is the more subtle and sneaky forms of religion that we may indeed be in bondage to. If we do not receive a proper vision of the present state of our surroundings, we cannot arise and leave it.

> **Where there is no vision, the people perish: but he that keepeth the law, happy is he (Proverbs 29:18).**

This text has often been interpreted to mean that a vision for ministry is necessary. If nothing is happening, the people perish. The next part, however, hints at a better interpretation. **He that keepeth the law, happy is he.** Here we see a connection between vision and keeping the law. This is not about being bound to the law. In the new covenant sense this would be better understood as keeping God's word.

Think of this in the sense of God's law written within the heart. It is not the law of Moses, or a code of ethics. It is not about religious observances. It is about His word abiding in you, and treasuring what He has said and done. It is the treasuring of His grace in Jesus.

It is through believing His word that you have become a new creation **(2Cor.5:17).** You have become a partaker of the **divine nature (2Peter 1:4).** You are married to another now **(Rom.7:4)**, and it is no longer you, but Christ who lives in you **(Gal.2:20)**!

Hard to believe, isn't it? But believe we must, even when we see all of our warts and failures. God is not looking at those outward things. He sees us spiritually in Christ, and we must learn to see this as well, **looking unto Jesus (Heb.12:2)** and not unto our shortcomings. Believers must have this vision in their lives, considering themselves **dead indeed unto sin but alive unto God through Jesus Christ our Lord (Rom.6:11).** Without having vision for this, the end result is a religion of formality, and we perish.

So many believers work so hard to obtain the truth of Christ living in them, working from the outside in and trying to get all their ducks in a row—so that Jesus can finally shine through them! It will never work that way! You have to start with the truth that you are dead to sin, and then rest in the fact that you are one with God in your spirit **(1Cor.6:17).** From there, your thoughts and actions will eventually fall into their proper place. There will be setbacks, but that does not change the spiritual reality. This is a very freeing truth to those who can grasp it. It comes by faith and not works.

Where do works come in? They come as a result from the vision. Take reading the Word, for example. People can read it without any vision, and as James describes, they are as **a man who looks at his natural face in a mirror; [who] once he has looked at himself and gone away, he has immediately forgotten what kind of person he was (James 1:23-4; NASB).** Believers can easily forget that they are a new creation and that God loves them just as if they had never sinned. It is easy to slip into reading the Bible as a mere religious obligation, because it is the right thing to do, or worse, because of the fear that God will be angry with you if you don't! Such reading yields little profit. But with vision, the Word has an awesome effect upon the soul. It transforms the believer, and as James concludes: **one who looks intently [with vision] at the perfect law, the law of liberty, and abides by it...this man shall be blessed in what he does (vs.25; NASB).** The one with vision experiences the law of liberty, and happy is he.

A good prayer before reading the word: **Open thou mine eyes, that I may behold wondrous things out of thy law (Ps.119:18).**

We still see through a glass darkly. There is always need for more vision, but be sure not to neglect what God has already given you. You have more vision than you realize, you just haven't believed it so much. Use what you have, and God will reveal more.

What does sin really look like? It is uglier than we know. If we do not get vision concerning this, we will not flee from sin as we should. What about heaven? It is glorious beyond our expectations! The glory of the Lord—just a glimpse of God is awesome! The more vision, the more we are drawn. We live by faith and not by sight, but without vision we perish!

The prodigals we have been discussing were perishing, until they received their vision and said, "Look at this mess I'm in!" What was once normal to them was suddenly undesirable. It was time to come out.

Not Without Action

The prodigal son did not just say, "What a mess!" and wallow in his pity. He did not try to adjust and hope for the best. He made a conscious decision to move, and he got up and left. It is not enough to be convicted or to bemoan the sour state of things. There must be the actual stepping forward in faith to get to the place of separation.

The account of the prodigal wife has not yet been concluded. We are not told that she made a move in this passage, only that she will. And thus, the Lord in His mercy says that He will lead her through a wilderness and draw her back to Himself (**Hosea 2:14**).God will go to such measures for us, even when we are hesitant and obstinate. But it is a rougher ride when we hold out. There is a wilderness to go through, or in Jonah's case, a fish's belly to languish in. Why waste the time? Consider the great mercy of God, and the dullness of staying in the same low conditions.

Will Rogers was known to have said, "Everybody's talking about the weather but nobody's doing anything about it!" There never seems to be any lack of words. Smith Wigglesworth once told someone who was saying all the right things, but obviously not trusting, "You don't have faith, you have language!" We need to be careful that we are not basing our spirituality only on our words. True faith will manifest itself in action.

When was the last time you sang, "I Surrender All"? Did you surrender all? This is not meant to condemn anyone. We all fall short and God's grace covers us. But I mention this simply to suggest we give more thought to our words, and try to follow up on them. It is noteworthy that the prodigal son said he would get up, and he did! Along the way, he gave careful thought to what else he would say: **"I will arise and go to my father, and will say unto him..." (Luke 15:18).**

Humility and Meekness

The vision has come and the move has been made. Now to present ourselves in the proper way. Not in arrogance, feeling proud of our accomplishment, but in truth. The prodigal son came with this in mind:

> **"Father, I have sinned against heaven, and before thee, I am no more worthy to be called thy son: make me as one of thy hired servants" (Luke 15:18-9).**

Those who come out in humility and meekness are truly different. The son did not think, "I have done the right thing, now perhaps I will be an example and everyone will buy my books!" No, he came content to be a servant. This is where the difference lies between being separate like the Pharisees and being separate in true holiness. True holiness looks to the Father rather than to the self.

The wonderful conclusion to the story is that the prodigal did not have to become like the hired servants. He didn't even have to say what he had prepared to say! Before he could speak a word, the father had run to embrace him. All it took was a turn towards his father.

There's no need to abase ourselves as the medieval monks did. There's no need to whine and cry that we are miserable sinners. If we have messed up, only one thing is required—that we turn back to God. The good news of the gospel is that we do not have to see ourselves as unworthy. There's no need to become like hired servants. The need is simply to turn, and the Father will come running to embrace us.

I'm glad the prodigal didn't say to him, "What are you doing? I have to do my penance first!"

Instead, I'll bet he was so thankful that He wanted to do nothing but please His forgiving father. That's how the gospel works. By faith, we receive God's forgiveness and love, and we become thankful. Then it becomes a joy to serve Him.

Every moment there is something to be thankful for, but this also requires vision. Every moment God's love is flowing towards us, but many stresses and pressures work to distract us. And so 'coming out' is not a one-time event, but requires a continual exercise of faith. It begins with a decision: "I am going to turn to God and His ways." Then it goes to action: actually turning to God and His ways! It is motivated by vision of what is good, and it is fueled by thankfulness—the response to His love, which the Bible says is beyond knowledge **(Eph.3:19).**

4. Coming Out in Fellowship

Even now we think and speak the same,
And cordially agree;
Connected all, through Jesus' name,
In perfect harmony

We all partake the joy of one,
The common peace we feel,
A peace to sensual minds unknown,
A joy unspeakable

And if our fellowship below
In Jesus be so sweet,
What heights of rapture shall we know,
When round His throne we meet!

---Charles Wesley

A GROUP OF CHRISTIANS were sitting around a big table and having a good time. They enjoyed chatting about their experiences of the day and laughed over some funny remarks while they ate. When the conversation died down for a moment, someone interjected, "I read a great passage this morning in Second Thessalonians, chapter one! It talked about the day when Jesus will be revealed from heaven—in blazing fire with His mighty angels. Have you ever really thought about that?"

"Yeah!" said another, "That's quite a passage! It really makes you stop and think how awesome it will be when He returns."

The first one continued, "It will be a greater display of glory than anything we have ever seen! I'm thankful for God's grace, that we can anticipate it and not fear."

"Amen. Just imagine seeing that, and then being received in love!" The two were lit up as they conversed for a while, and then there was silence.

The others at the table did not know what to say. One gave something of an affirming, "Hmm. Yeah." Another seemed to have missed it, being so engrossed in his food. Still another wore a blank expression on her face. And the silence lingered a moment.

"So what are you doing tomorrow?" one person asked. Then the conversation revived, and the group became a-buzz with plans for the coming weekend.

Spiritual encouragement often gets snuffed out by the conversation of the mundane. We find ourselves sinking under the waters of temporal or trivial concerns and miss the blessing of meeting together in the conversation of Christ. In the scenario above, the two talkers found themselves breathing some fresh air for a little while until they were pulled back under by the plans for the weekend. I believe many would like to talk about spiritual things, but often do not know how.

Some Christians can 'swim' the waters of sweet fellowship better than others. Put them together and they will talk for hours, building each other up and encouraging each other in the Lord. Sometimes you can just meet another Christian and wind up talking with them like you've known them all your life.

Others would enjoy this kind of fellowship but it does not come so easily. They float for a while, but would readily swim better if they could.

Meanwhile there are some who rarely if ever make it to the top, who seem to just move whichever way the tide carries them.

Then there are those like the Plecostomus, a fish commonly placed in aquariums that dwells on the bottom and sucks up all the algae. These folks suck up all the world's rotten outgrowth and seem to have no convictions about it at all.

The hymn above by Charles Wesley gives an exciting contrast. Fellowship should be spiritual, if it is to be good. The benefits reaped include enjoying the presence of Jesus Himself, and the building up of the saints. We find refreshment in this. 'Non-spiritual' fellowship can be enjoyed as well, but it does not reach the joy unspeakable found here.

While existing in these earthen vessels (2Cor.4:7), however, it is easier to stay within the mundane. That is why it is necessary to make an effort to go higher. Most of the time, spiritual fellowship doesn't just happen, and it certainly shouldn't be forced. Nonetheless, attempts can be made to come out, or swim to the top, in order to be reinvigorated by the fresh air and light of the Holy Spirit.

Why let the devil rob us of the best? We cannot force anointed conversations, but we can do our part to get in a position that allows the Holy Spirit to participate. The goal is to seek out ways to encourage one another in the Lord. The mistake is to get too complacent with the mundane.

Good spiritual fellowship is strengthening and uplifting. Most Christians want this, yet fail to get it because no attempt is made and so many other items are focused on in conversation.

Let's Talk About the Movies

Take movies, for example. Some people just love to talk about the films they have seen. Not all of them are bad, and sometimes it is good conversation. But when that is all there is, entertainment can become a god. Faces light up as favorite scenes are recalled, and fellowship centers around an industry that puts out more evil than good.

Movies grab our attention because they are sensational—that is, geared toward our senses. They are romantic escapes from reality and they stimulate the emotions. Usually there is little need to think. Because they are of this nature, they provide a nice diversion from the stress of daily life. It is understandable that we are drawn to them.

The Christian, however, is called above the senses, and above the world. Therefore, we should be very careful about how much credence we give to films and celebrities. A film can be an enjoyable experience, and sometimes even meaningful. I am not suggesting it is always a sin to watch one! However, if we are pressing on to live a higher spiritual experience, we will desire to be less effected by the charms and allurements coming from Hollywood.

There is freedom and grace. You can watch what you want, but hopefully you are sensitive to the things that are contrary to God. Many Christians don't seem to mind. They applaud and recommend films that promote so much wrong:

"Oh, that movie was very good, except that it had a lot of bad language."

"You'll really like this one. It's a little violent, but it is so good!"

"I thought it was great, but I had to shut my eyes during the sex scenes."

They may not agree with the elements that are questionable, but it is likely that they are still affected by them to some degree. **Romans 12:2 says, "Be not conformed to this world but be ye transformed by the renewing of your mind."** To be conformed takes no effort at all. In fact, it means to be molded to the shape or image of the world. Unless you take charge and guard your heart, the world influence just does what it wants with you. Continual exposure to ungodliness makes it gradually seem more normal. Or, it at least makes it harder to think on higher things.

To be transformed means to be changed. It is a metamorphosis, like that of the caterpillar to the butterfly. It is also something that just happens to you, but it requires an effort on your part to renew your mind. Most efforts are misplaced—we try to change ourselves, always trying to do better and rarely making progress. We can't change ourselves! It is God who transforms us. Our efforts should instead be focused on renewing our minds- changing the way we think according to the Word of God. Then we will find that our tastes have changed. Our actions will flow from how we think. That is why I am very picky about what I allow on my TV screen.

"Well!" One objects, "My faith can handle it. If that kind of stuff offends you, you are just the weaker brother mentioned in Romans 14!"

Please take a look at **Romans 14.** It is a chapter concerning traditions, or the ceremonial aspects of the law. Questionable films present a moral issue. Romans 14 does not suggest that the stronger faith will be more comfortable in immoral situations. When a film continually blasphemes the name of God we are right in the midst of that immoral situation. The one who seeks purity and desires communion with the Holy Spirit cannot, or at least *should not* feel comfortable with that or anything else that would grieve Him.

Imagine going to a foreign country and watching their films. Let's suppose their films were riddled with anti-American (or anti-wherever you are from) propaganda and blatant disregard for your ways. Add the insults and the mocking of those who are dearest to you. Wouldn't you be sick of it after a while? Why then do you tolerate all of Hollywood's affronts to your King and your heavenly citizenship?

Granted we have to deal with this world as long as we are in this world, and there are films that have some redeeming value in spite of their corruption. No one is going to be ruined or condemned by watching something questionable. But a continual diet of it is bound to have negative effects on the spiritual life.

What films are acceptable then? That is for you to decide. I decide like this- I may view a film just as I may stay and chat with a group of secular people in a public place. I wouldn't expect them to be completely in accordance with my values. But if I began to hear that the conversation was getting too unsavory, I would probably try to change the subject or leave. If I saw them begin to do something obscene, I would get as far as possible. Certainly if they were in my house, I would ask them to leave. Most people would do the same, yet those same rude acts and language are accepted on their own video screens.

This should not be a legalistic matter. I know the reality of our love for entertainment, and I am not completely immune. My point, though, is that we should make it a goal to get farther from it. The problem, I believe, is in the undue esteem. Let's not be legalistic, but let's consider such entertainment a weakness more than a treat.

A careful check will keep movies in their place. Talking about the movies can be enjoyable. Only make sure that the heart is not enamored with Hollywood. Seek to be more enamored with God's Kingdom.

Let's Talk About Sports

There are many excellent qualities about sports. We can be thankful to God for the variety of recreational activities available. Competition can be quite healthy, and a good game is always good entertainment (if your team wins).

But here we need vision. Something awful has happened in the sports world. An attitude has crept in. "Image is everything," said one, but the message is everywhere. Hard rock music has wedded itself to sports broadcasts. Advertising has exploited athletes and the games. Don't forget gambling and all the alcohol ads.

Without a doubt, a very common problem is the almost religious bondage in the sports world. "I can't miss the game!!!"

One communication philosopher remarked on the secular religion of sports. Consider the fellowship that can occur between complete strangers in common interest over last week's game. Statistics are remembered like Scriptures. The altar is the television. There are holidays, like Super Bowl Sunday.

This, of course, does not apply to all sports fans in such a negative manner, but it is taken to extremes in many cases.

Some people's whole day is ruined if their team loses an important game. Hear how people get riled up and shout at the games. "C'mon!!!

Aw, you stink!!" From what spirit does this arise? Probably not from meekness and humility. Some may object that it is just in fun, and if so, okay. But check the faces sweating and red as they rant and scream at their teams. Something more than fun may be present.

I mention this so that we can exercise caution in our sports interests. Like the movies, we should not give them an undue position in our hearts. Sports may be more dangerous, however, because they are not as visibly immoral. It is easy to be deceived and think that fanaticism is okay because it is 'just sports.' The sports world is NOT innocent. This is not to say that everyone involved is deceived. There are Christian athletes who bring glory to God. But the general atmosphere in professional sports is one of sensationalism and seduction. Enjoy the game, but avoid the shame!

Please remember, I am not saying that these topics are taboo for Christians, or that they should never watch a film or game together. I am suggesting we approach them with awareness and that we remember who we are, people of the Kingdom.

It does not hurt to review the great plays of a game or a great scene in a film, but it does hurt when that is all there is. And of course, sports and films are not the only areas that we go astray to. The real matter concerns how much we give of our hearts to anything outside of God.

The issue at hand is whether or not we will desire to find our social gatherings spiritually encouraging, just as we would seek spiritual encouragement in our alone times with God. We may be growing individually, but don't let the devil distract us from growing together as well.

Howdy Partner

I think it is a mistake to call any time with other believers 'fellowship.' Just because we gather over a meal does not mean that we really connect with one another.

The word 'fellowship' is derived from the Greek word, koinonos, which means 'partner,' and from koinoneo, which means 'to share.' If we would come out in our fellowship, consider the holy partnership between Christ and His church. It is a family relationship. In any fellowship situation, we should view each other as partners along the way to our Kingdom destination. We shouldn't be afraid to offer encouragement or pray for each other if it seems like a good time.

We don't have to impose a 'religious service' on every social gathering, but we need not fear expressing our delights in Jesus and His Word. We might have many common trivial interests, but when we express deep interest in Jesus and His Word, we spur one another on to love and good works. We perceive Him better because we have invited Him into the conversation. The result is strength and joy—fuel for the walk of faith that can otherwise be more of a struggle.

Will we focus our partnership on the trivial and mundane? That is not 'sweet fellowship.' When gathering together, make an effort to look for any opening that might allow for the Spirit's joining into the conversation. If alert, we might find an opportunity to really build one another up and be mutually edified.

Again, fellowship cannot be forced. Don't let the enemy turn you into a legalist and make you frown on every interaction without substance. If a conversation never gets there, at least our hearts can be there. We can rest in His presence and love the others we are with, even if it is only over the food. But I hope the church aspires to higher things. This is important for coming out in any aspect of the faith.

5. Coming Out with Joy

> **For ye shall go out with joy, and be led forth with peace: the mountains and the hills shall break forth before you into singing, and all the trees of the field shall clap their hands.**
> **(Isaiah 55:12).**

IT IS A PRIVILEGE to serve the Lord in China. In spite of the difficult environment, the blessings have been many. One December, it was a real treat to go high up into some remote mountains, visit a school for village children, and sing Christmas hymns for them. With several friends, some guitars and an accordion, we sang "Joy to the World" and others. Though the children did not understand our English, they sat mesmerized as they watched and heard sounds completely foreign to them.

The officials hosting us did not understand our English either, but they knew we were singing of God's love. One official (to our surprise) even began to declare to the children that we were there in the name of God, and that "it is clear that Christmas has something to do with peace and happiness!" He told the children that God loved them. We had talked to him before, but we were amazed that he was so affected and blurting these things out before other communist officials!

The Spirit of God was there. This man was clearly touched. The children were happy. And as we sang, the joy of heaven filled our souls. I knew it showed on our faces. The earth groans waiting for the redemption (Romans 8:22), but it seemed that day as if the mountains and the hills broke forth into shouts of joy!

This illustrates the power of separation. It is not in words, but in joy. Up on that mountain we were quite separated from the mainstream of the world. And as foreigners in that land, we were obviously separated identities from the villagers. But the power came in with our joy as we sang praises to God in their midst.

True Happiness

Some people think that holiness is a somber business, and that it is no fun to come out and be separate. This idea likely comes from associations with others who have been harsh and legalistic. But true holiness must be accompanied with joy. True holiness brings us out with joy and leads us forth with peace. How can it be otherwise? We were made to belong to God. When we abide in our calling and live consecrated lives unto Him, how can we not be happy?

You see, it is the sin and conformity to this world that ties us to the curse. Under the curse, we fall prey to the troubles and problems that result from fallen life on earth. But when we separate ourselves unto God, we rise above the curse. The problems won't necessarily go away, but this alleviates many struggles and produces happiness. The pursuit of this happiness means endeavoring to come out farther and farther from the ways of the common, and to enter more and more into the joy of the Lord.

Where to Find Joy

Romans 15:13 says, **Now the God of hope fill you with all joy and peace in believing...** Joy doesn't just come upon us. It usually doesn't work just to pray, "God please give me joy." Joy (as well as peace) comes through believing. It is faith in God and His promises that bring rejoicing. Look at how Isaiah rejoiced believing the truths of salvation and righteousness:

> **I will greatly rejoice in the LORD, my soul shall be joyful in my God; for he hath clothed me with the garments of salvation, he hath covered me with the robe of right-**

eousness, as a bridegroom decketh himself with ornaments, and as a bride adorneth herself with her jewels (Isaiah 61:10).

What do you believe about yourself? Do you believe you are just a "sinner saved by grace" and that you can't help but fall into the traps of the world? Or do you believe that you have been clothed with the garments of salvation and covered with the robe of righteousness? As a man thinks, so is he (**Proverbs 23:7**). If you really believe the wonderful truths and promises of God, it will put a smile on your face and a bounce in your step (if that's not your personality, then it will at least draw you closer unto God).

Think about it—apart from Christ you were naked. Now consider being brought before His throne, to eternity's door. Yet He has covered you! Instead of shame, you become glorified! When this truly becomes vision, it leads to rejoicing, even in the most desperate of times. It fuels a walk of faith in victory, and shines as wedding ornaments and jewels. And look at how God brings about His witness through this:

For as the earth bringeth forth her bud, and as the garden causeth the things that are sown in it to spring forth, so the Lord GOD will cause righteousness and praise to spring forth before all nations (vs.11).

Vision is needed for this as well. In the natural sense it seems that holy lives are often disregarded. Persecution is also a common consequence. In the spiritual realm, however, the kingdom advances. In some cases the witness is manifested, as in our Chinese official. Praise seemed to spring forth from him. Ultimately, God will use His people to cause righteousness and praise to spring forth before all nations. This is the hope of the Kingdom.

Not Without Faith

Faith is necessary for joyful holiness. It might be considered in three respects:

• *A trusting faith* in the atoning work of Christ. This humbles us and enables us to receive His love and joy. There is no stewing over sin, because we believe **it is finished (John 19:30).** In faith we look to Jesus as the source of our righteousness, and not to our works. Nonetheless, a trusting faith should result in:

• *An active faith* that steps out according to the Word. If we really believe, we will live accordingly. God will then do wonders through us. Though temptations abound, an active faith should be accompanied with:

• *An expectant faith* of the glory to come, and even of the glory that is now in process. This supports us as we desire to live for Him, just as Jesus **who for the joy that was set before Him endured the cross (Heb.12:2).**

Without holiness, no one will see the Lord (**Heb.12:14**). But no one can live holy without having faith. Holiness is the work of God in our lives, and any outward success comes from Him. But here is a surprising fact: we are *already* holy in Christ Jesus! Looking at the flesh and the reasoning of the mind will suggest that this isn't true, but faith will instead cling to verses like **2 Corinthians 5:21**, which reveals that we have **been made the righteousness of God in Him.**

There is **joy and peace in believing (Romans 15:13)!** But most believers do not believe they have become the righteousness of God. They are still self-absorbed in their outward progress or lack thereof. Believing the spiritual reality of who we are in Christ will take away such considerations about progress. This has a way of bringing joy and turning our hearts away from the world. It is one thing to be separate in an air of legalism. It is quite another to be separate in order to guard the joy that comes from faith. And after having enjoyed sweet fellowship with God, the things of the world just don't seem as desirable. **Thou hast put gladness in my heart, more than in the time that their corn and their wine increased (Psalm 4:7).**

Do you know this gladness? Why settle for the pleasures of the world's corn and wine? There is a greater gladness available. Will you take the steps of faith and remove yourself from the idea of making religious progress? Will you believe that you are already righteous, and act upon it?

A greater joy will greet you. Be filled with the Holy Spirit, delving into the truth, believing and receiving His promises, and acting on them. Then the fruit will manifest. The fruit of the Spirit is healthy. Why settle for the 'tooth-rotting candy' of the world? Let's set our sights for the gold, knowing not just what God wants from us, but the blessings behind it all.

And we will go out with joy and be led forth in peace!

6. Coming Out to Serve

SERVICE WITH A SMILE! We all appreciate it when help comes from a friendly worker. The one who 'serves with a smile' blesses both the one he is serving and himself. He misses the blessing, though, if the smile is not sincere.

When I was in college, I worked at a fancy restaurant for a summer. An elderly lady worked there as a waitress. She really knew her craft. When the customers came in, she turned on the charm. She mingled with them as she took their orders. She smiled and said, "OK, sweetie," when they made special requests. She complied like a caring grandmother.

Her countenance changed, however, when she returned to her station out of their sight. She became Mrs. Hyde, cussing and complaining about the customers! She bemoaned her troubles and hated her job. She knew the art of getting her tips, but inside she was the poorest of all the waitresses there.

> **And if I give all my possessions to feed the poor, and if I deliver my body to be burned, but do not have love, it profits me nothing (1Cor.13:3; NASB).**

This woman did not like her job, and as long as she continued in this vain she would never enjoy it.

In contrast, I had a Chinese student who was told in high school that his English was very poor. He was bitter about this, but as a determined young man he chose to continue his studies in Foreign Languages. He came into the college telling his classmates that he hated English but (in order to spite those who told him he was no good) he was going to work hard at it. As he applied himself, he confessed that he was beginning to enjoy it.

Both the waitress and the student had ill thoughts toward their vocation, but one chose to rise above the negative and began to see the positive.

The Christian is blessed with a greater window into the positive. Whatever the circumstances, the Christian has a great hope in knowing that **all things work together for good to them that love God, to them who are the called according to His purpose. (Rom. 8:28)**. This doesn't mean that God causes all things to happen, and it doesn't mean that all things are good. But it means that He can turn even the bad situations around and bless His people through them. When this is grasped, those situations no longer have the rule over our hearts, and the peace of God can enter in.

Some people fear that God will call them to a strange country, a jungle or a swamp to serve Him. It is unlikely. **Psalm 37:4** says that He will give you the desires of your heart. You don't need to fear. Jonah feared going to Ninevah, but He didn't have the Holy Spirit living in him the way new covenant believers do today. If Christ lives in you, He will put it into your heart to do His will. Yet even for Jonah, God had his best in mind. God's thoughts toward us are **thoughts of peace and not of evil (Jer.29:11)**. To remember this is to go into service with a smile.

But Jonah sulked under a gourd. Like that old waitress, he returned to his station in a sour frame of mind: **"I do well to be angry even unto death!" (Jonah 4:9)**. He had just seen revival come through his preaching, and that should make any minister happy. But since he didn't really want to see Ninevah revived, he sacrificed joy for selfishness.

A key to growing in Christ is learning to separate oneself from selfish interests. God wants us to come out refreshed from the gourd He has provided, rather than selfishly keep to ourselves. We do no good as Christians if we do no good to others.

Cheerful giving

> **But just as you excel in everything- in faith, in speech, in knowledge, in complete earnestness. . . see that you also excel in this grace of giving (2 Cor. 8:7; NIV)**

Though this was spoken in the context of taking up a collection for the poor, it must also be considered in the sense of giving our very selves, just like Jesus Christ, who **was rich, yet for your sakes He became poor, that ye through His poverty might be rich (vs.9).**

There are many in the church and throughout history who have excelled in faith, preaching, learning, or earnestness. The sincerity of love, however, is tested and proved in GIVING (**2 Cor.8:8**). Jesus's whole ministry can be characterized as giving. **The Son of Man did not come to be served, but to serve, and to give His life a ransom for many (Matt.20:28; NASB).** This should spur us on to do the same.

It takes faith to sow a seed and expect the fruit. The Lord has even implied that He will bless us without sowing and reaping (**Matt. 6:26**)! There is a principle, though, that promises a return on seeds sown. Consider these great promises:

> **Bring ye all the tithes into the storehouse, that there may be meat in mine house, and prove me now herewith, saith the LORD of hosts, if I will not open you the windows of heaven, and pour you out a blessing, that there shall not be room enough to receive it (Malachi 3:10).**

And again:

> **Give, and it shall be given unto you; good measure, pressed down, and shaken together, and running over, shall men give into your bosom. For with the same measure that ye mete withal it shall be measured to you again (Luke 6:38).**

These promises should not be taken in a greedy sense, but they should bring cheerfulness into our offerings. Whether we give money or service, it is not a somber occasion of loss but a happy occasion of divine investment. But the flesh gets in the way all the time. It would rather receive. "What about me?" It cries. It only looks at the cost. Sometimes we may shy away from serving others in difficult situations because we fear the costs involved. But often such costs bring in the greatest blessings.

"I have meat to eat that ye know not of," said Jesus **(John 4:32)**. This is the meat that truly delights the soul. We can stay in our pantries and snack on the frivolous bits that life has to offer, or we can find joy even as Jesus did, and say like Him, **"My meat is to do the will of Him that sent me, and to finish his work" (vs.34).**

His Will be Done

A word of balance—don't approach service as a glutton! The walk of faith is more about *being* than *doing.* Some believers get so caught up in works without ever entering into His rest. It is also easy to put on a sort of 'religious ambition' and do works that should never really be attempted. Sometimes an idea or proposition for service can look good on the surface, like a peace treaty with the Gibeonites (**Joshua 9**), but later turn out to be a thorn in the side. Any other meat besides 'the will of Him that sent me' will likely result in (pardon the puns here) spiritual indigestion. The work will tire the flesh and fail to nourish like that which is empowered by God.

If you know that God is calling you to something—go for it! Don't let circumstances frighten you away from what He has in mind. He will see you through. He will bless your sacrifices. It is most fulfilling to be in the place you know God wants you to be.

"But I don't know what He's calling me to, and I'm not sure I am in the right place even now." There is no condemnation in Christ and God can bless you wherever you are. His will is not a puzzle that He holds us responsible for. He will reveal it clearly in due time. In the meantime there is freedom to just follow Him where we are.

To those who know without a doubt what God wants, but run like Jonah, I believe there is new covenant grace to cover even that. They don't need to fear that something bad will happen because they chose a different direction. But they may miss out on certain glories, and God may call someone else in their place.

Gladys Aylward was a missionary to China in the early 1900's. To say that her story is remarkable is an understatement.

Working as a parlor maid in London, she was convinced she was called to bring the Gospel to China. Rejected by the local mission organization, she saved her money until she could travel alone by train, and this was in the middle of tension and fighting between China and the Soviet Union.

She became fluent in the Chinese language and helped run an inn with an older missionary woman. The older woman died, and Gladys Aylward continued the work. She met an official in the area and became very influential (he later became a Christian). When the evil practice of footbinding had been outlawed, she was given the responsibility to go into villages and inspect feet. This gave her the opportunity to bring the Gospel to many in the countryside. She found and adopted a number of abandoned children, and that number continued to grow.

In the spring of 1938, Japanese bombers invaded her territory. Fleeing from the attack, she led about 100 orphans on a 12-day journey across the mountains. Their goal was to get safely to an orphanage across the Yellow River. Some nights were spent in the open air. They trekked in the midst of war and a deluge of bombs bursting nearby.

When they finally got to the river, there was no way to cross it! Gladys Aylward and the children all knelt down to pray and sing, seeking God for the impossible. A Chinese officer eventually heard the singing and found them. He was able to arrange for a boat, and they crossed over to safety!

Miss Aylward was said to have collapsed after this experience. The war had gotten to her and she caught typhus fever as well. A few years later she returned to England for her health's sake. She had gained some fame there, and said something very interesting to one interviewer:

> "I wasn't God's first choice. It must have been a man- a wonderful man. A well-educated man. I don't know what happened. Perhaps he wasn't willing...And God looked down...and saw Gladys Aylward."[*]

Gladys Aylward knew about the meat of doing God's will, and nothing could stop her from going on to do it. Who was that man, though, who didn't come out? He missed some great troubles to be sure, but he also missed the glory. God touched many lives through Gladys, and even more glory is laid up for her in the age to come! Whatever service we are called to, the trials we persevere through will shine like jewels in a future crown. The thought of this should help bring about service with a smile. If God could even use a little London parlor maid, He could use people like you and me!

---

[*] From the book, *From Jerusalem to Irian Jaya,* p.254.

7. Coming Out of a Rut

AS A FOREIGN LANGUAGE teacher, I can tell you about the challenges of keeping things interesting in the classroom. Most teachers will agree that variety is very important. Students simply respond better to creativity. The greatest danger occurs when the course becomes predictable. Students can grow weary or fall into a state of adaptation, which language teaching expert, James Asher, defined as "the phenomenon in which one discontinues making a response to a continual stimulus." That is, one may participate in the process without really learning anything. There is still a stimulus, or action involved, but the mind has shifted into automatic. A good teacher will be very careful to see that this does not happen in class.

If this is necessary in the realms of education, how much more is it in our spiritual education? Here I mean that we as Christians are learners in the school of God. We are also responsible for the oversight of our spiritual walks. Therefore it is necessary to take great care that we don't fall into a spiritual state of adaptation.

It is a sad reflection on the state of a church when its services are boring. A congregation should be led into the presence of God, to worship Him and to hear from Him. We know that when we come into the actual presence of the Lord in the Kingdom it will be anything BUT boring! There will be no sleepy heads before His throne! Down here though, adaptation has infiltrated many a body of believers.

So many church services can become stale because of repeated routines. Leaders can become so busy that they do not have time to plan anything different. Or, they are inhibited by others who refuse to change. Some folks find the repetition quite comfortable. They know what to expect and it satisfies their religious requirements. But they should not be satisfied!

When thou saidst, Seek ye my face; my heart said unto thee, Thy face, LORD, will I seek (Psalm 27:8).

A characteristic of a Christian should be this: he or she is one who seeks the Lord's face. Not just a one time, "I got it!" kind of deal, but a continuous seeking of His face in every situation. **For now we see through a glass darkly (1Cor. 13:12),** we know only in part. As the Lord told Joshua, there is more land to be taken (Joshua 13:1). To get complacent with our present state is to fall into adaptation. The best land lies before us. The spiritually abundant life of Christ will manifest more fully as He is passionately pursued. But to kick into adaptation is to invite weariness.

So how can we keep ourselves passionate? Just asking the Lord to help may not be enough. He will indeed renew your strength (**Isaiah 40:31**), but your waiting on Him must be active, not passive. As Paul told Timothy, it is necessary to stir things up (**2Tim.1:6**).

Newness in Christ

I know a university professor who used to advise his class, "When you go home, try taking a different route every now and then. Even if it takes a little longer, it's good for you!" This wise teacher knew the value of incorporating 'newness' into a world of routines:

--Taking a different route home would bring fresh scenery to the eyes.

--It would require an added alertness.

--Some deliberation would be needed to go the different way.

--Whether it was a smooth trip or not, it would have to at least be a little more interesting than usual.

--New sights might be discovered along the way.

A simple change like this would quicken the senses and stir up some life where adaptation had been setting in. Newness always calls us to attention.

When the believer is converted to Jesus, he is made new. **Therefore if any man be in Christ, he is a new creature: old things are passed away; behold, all things are become new (2Cor.5:17).** When Jesus is first received as Lord and Savior there is often an exhilarating joy. The believer has literally passed from death to life, and is drawn to this sweet new relationship with God. But that is not the end of it. Behold, all things are become new! All things are made *fresh* (as the Greek would imply). If any man BE IN Christ, there is newness, whether it is at conversion or after years of following Jesus. The great danger is to wander out of the 'fresh' and into a rut.

Jesus said, **"I am come that they might have life, and that they might have it more abundantly" (John 10:10).** The Greek here might be better translated, "might keep on having life, and keep on having it abundantly." There are seasons we go through that require extra perseverance, but if the general scope of your walk with Jesus has been less than abundant, it is time to **kindle afresh the gift of God which is in you (2 Tim.1:6; NASB).** It is time to stir up those stagnant waters. It is time to take a 'fresh route home.' Here are some suggestions…

Ways to Break the Rut

The first step in breaking out of a rut is *to recognize that there is a rut.* This requires humility, because pride can blind many eyes to the fact that their Christian experience has become stale. Pride can cling to traditions and routines and cite those as evidence of life. It will hide behind works and words. It takes humility to hunger and thirst. But God lifts up the humble, and they that hunger and thirst shall be filled.

The next step in breaking out of a rut is *to turn away from any known sin.* Sin keeps us from enjoying God's fullness. God's love is like the finest of wines, poured into the cup of our hearts. Because Jesus paid it all, you can still enjoy His love, even with the presence of sin, but that stain or blemish in the cup inhibits the full enjoyment of its flavor. Through Christ, God loves us just the same, but turning away from sin will remove that which hinders our enjoyment of Him.

Sin gives Satan an inroad into your life, and he is the thief who comes to steal, kill, and destroy (**John 10:10**). Satan also will dull your heart to the things of God. Sin just isn't in our best interest. **Romans 6:16** says, **Know ye not, that to whom ye yield yourselves servants to obey, his servants ye are to whom ye obey; whether of sin unto death, or of obedience unto righteousness?**

Repentance is an easy way out of sin's strongholds. Repentance simply means turning away from sin and toward God. If you feel you have blown it in major proportions, just repent like you did when you first came to God. Remember the prodigal son. All it took was a turn in the right direction and his father accepted him. Maybe you haven't blown it big time, but you just know that there are little compromises and failures in your life. Just turn to the Father. The devil would rather you mope and beat yourself up. Instead, turn, knowing that you are already **accepted in the Beloved (Eph.1:6)**. God loves us no less when we are in the mud with the pigs. But we can't experience His love until we get up and GO TO HIM. Remember, the father ran to embrace His returning son (Luke 15:20).

As each day brings with it a new morning, it is good to go to the Lord with a renewed devotion. Think again on God's love for you.

Along the same lines as repentance, a valuable step in breaking out of a rut is *to return to the place of life.* Think back on the times that you were spiritually excited. Think back on your conversion or awakening to the things of God. I find it helpful to keep a journal and go back and remind myself of how God has worked in my life. If you cannot find any great works to be reminded of, go back and study the lives and works of other great men and women of God. The spirituality of the past has often outshined our present day devotion.

Set apart time to enjoy God's presence. We all can enter that special sense of His presence if we are patient. But it is not necessary to always have a good feeling. We can rejoice that He is here *even if we cannot feel it.* Go back to the Word and start believing the promises and taking them personally. When it says He shall never leave you nor forsake you **(Heb.13:5),** read it as and receive it as "He shall never leave ME nor forsake ME." He is here! It doesn't matter what I feel. Feelings are important, but they come and go. God's word remains consistent and true whether the feelings are there or not. Believing this keeps me from falling apart whenever it seems that "God has left." I know He hasn't.

Another way to come out of the rut is to read the book of Acts and *aspire to the same power and gifts that the early church had.* When a prophet lost the borrowed ax head, Elisha instructed him to go back to the place where it fell (**2 Kings 6:6**). He recovered it there. I heard a preacher use this example to exhort us to go back to Pentecost and seek the promise of the Holy Spirit. If we would be an effective church, we need that same 'power from on high.'

Get baptized in the Holy Spirit. We see so little of 'Acts type of power' today because of extreme unbelief and a very materialistic culture. Don't be prejudiced or afraid of the gifts of the Spirit. Our pride keeps us from submitting to His power. Our pride keeps us worrying more about how we might be branded "a fanatic". This is 'rut' worry. To get out of a rut it may be best to follow David's example and say, **"I will be even more undignified than this" (2Sam.6:22;** NKJV**).** I'm not saying to make a show of yourself, but you can at least in private throw out all inhibitions and worship the Lord.

In coming out of the rut, it is helpful *to turn away from the things of our society that hamper faith or hinder hope.* Stop reading books that foster doubt. Don't be so glued to the news and all the doomsday reports. The Lord is your God, and He will see you through the times. Turn away from the music that sends a negative or ungodly message.

I had some friends that loved 'Christian music' that contained nothing but griping and complaining. "It's real life, man!" We could all appreciate the honesty of the artists' struggles. We might wallow with them! But I am suggesting we reject that and find a message that helps pull us out.

I was really feeling down one time before leaving the States back for China. We went to a church service and sang, "A Mighty Fortress is our

God." At that time, the truth in that hymn just rushed over me and strengthened my heart. Misery loves company, but it is the truth that sets us free!

"But I've sang that a hundred times and never felt a rush!" Maybe, but next time think about what you are singing. It is easy to just sing words, and the more familiar they are, the easier it is to go about it mindlessly. High and lofty truths may be expressed in worship without ever giving thought to what they really mean. The key to worshiping God in song is to **sing ye praises with understanding (Ps.47:7).** But I have digressed.

Another way to get out of the rut is *to call a friend.* If there is someone you can relate to on a spiritual level, the fellowship will do you good. Often, however, it is quite tempting to never call during the down times. There is no motivation, and the devil wants to keep you away. He knows there is reviving power in good fellowship, so he places doubts about whether you should call or not. Or, it may be *pride* that keeps you away. Nobody likes to confess that they need some help or support.

Maybe you are down because you have no such friends. Jesus knows what it is like to be lonely. He was so often misunderstood. His friends slept as He desired them to pray. They also left Him as the soldiers came to take Him away.

Cling to the truth that God cares for you (**1Peter 5:7**). God's love surpasses knowledge, and it surpasses the situations you are going through. Change is always ahead. If nobody else cares, God has moved heaven and earth to call you His beloved. The devil would try to blind you and cause you to lapse into hopelessness. But God is a **God of hope (Rom.15:13).** Seek first His kingdom and His righteousness, and then "all these things" shall be added unto you (**Matthew 6:33**). They are in one sense already yours.

Theological Rut

Maybe there is weariness because there has been more of a relationship with teachings and traditions than with the Lord Himself. Seminaries will make their students read thousands of pages within a limited time frame in order to get a good grade. How can they be spiritually fed when they are rushing and skimming through just to meet a requirement? It all gets into the head, but it is soon forgotten.

Many blogs and websites argue and debate theology, calling anyone who disagrees with them a heretic. People are so tied to their systems and theological affiliations that they hardly reflect any witness of a relationship that loves God Himself and their neighbor. It is all about exposing error and being right!

I'm so glad that God is not grading us on theological accuracy. I'm not saying we shouldn't care about doctrine, though. I'm just trying to suggest we focus more on the PERSON and exhibit Christ's love to the world. That is more important than proving that I am right and you are wrong about something.

So how about going out and working *to be a blessing to someone*? This will get you out of a rut. Get involved with a good ministry, or do something nice for your neighbor. Give your parents a call. Visit someone in the hospital or in jail.

Coming out of a rut requires *commitment*. Sometimes it is not a quick fix. If you are going to mine for gold, you are going to have to work hard to get it. The American fast food mentality will not do for spiritual growth. But as a believer who wants the best, a serious investment of your time and focus will pay off.

Look at the serious businessman of the world. See how he works overtime to make his money. See how he studies his Wall Street Journal so that he can stay informed and on top of everything. See him calling his stockbroker and reading books that will teach him how to earn more money. How many spend their lives in the office, working overtime just to get ahead. And it's all for that which is temporary and can't truly satisfy. What we have is of much greater and lasting value, but we could learn from the businessman's diligence.

And so, here is an important step for breaking out of the rut: *get excited!* Look to the joy set before those who are diligent, and anticipate getting to know Jesus better. God will promote us into the higher realms of the spiritual life.

It may be useful to begin pushing your excitement. You may not feel excited, but the sticks must be rubbed together if there is to be any flame. The heavenly fire might catch the small offering up of your sparks.

Get excited about the Lord, though the 'Michal' spirit may oppress and brandish you for being undignified (**2 Sam. 6:16**). Come against that in prayer, worship, and perseverance. Stand firm against the enemy that would rob you of joy. All things are new, and even this moment is new.

Step out of the rut, starting…NOW!

8. One Place NOT to Come Out Of

> **But thou, when thou prayest, enter into thy closet, and when thou hast shut thy door, pray to thy Father which is in secret; and thy Father which seeth in secret shall reward thee openly (Matthew 6:6).**

WHAT WE DO IN SECRET speaks a lot about our true spirituality. The heart of the Christian faith is the Christian faith within the heart. It is the secret abiding in Christ, the desire for His kingdom and the communion with the Spirit that make a real difference. Even the heathen pray (vs.7), and the religions of the world make a show of their prayers. But the Christian enters into a secret place where the focus can be on God alone.

Here is the paradox for this chapter: we must enter in, in order to come out. It is in prayer that the life of God is boosted in His people. In this verse, the Greek for 'closet' could also be translated as 'store-room.' It is in this store-room that we accumulate the hidden treasures of God's friendship and love, and this in turn adds luster to the light that Jesus shines in our lives.

Shut the Door!

One reason why prayer seems to look better on paper than in the actual doing is because we often 'enter into the closet' but fail to 'shut the door.' That is, we come to pray but we come with a multitude of extraneous thoughts. We have other plans in mind and our responsibilities beckon.

Then the devil throws in his two cents and makes plenty of suggestions or temptations. There are also the many physical distractions that make it hard to get quiet in an increasingly busy society.

It is hard to shut the door, but it is necessary. It requires an act of the will. Every thought and distraction must be rejected in order to get into that secret place of divine communion with God. These distractions will continue to knock, but the will that shuts the door finds the happy place of heavenly solitude.* Then, like in other aspects of the spiritual journey, the Lord will meet us and carry us the rest of the way. "You have made it through the trials and obstacles, now enjoy my presence." When this happens, prayer becomes desirable and it is often hard to break away.

Like all that we have been discussing, the supernatural is required in prayer. Weariness occurs when prayer becomes a mere duty of the flesh. Then routine becomes a rut, and the prayers seem to bounce off the ceiling. It is time for renewed faith and a fresh approach.

Here is what I have found helpful for building up the prayer life…

Newness in Prayer

Saturate yourself with the Word of God. Pray before, during, and after reading. This will reveal the mind of Christ and transform you as it renews your mind. Read the Bible consistently. **"If ye abide in me, and my words abide in you, ye shall ask what ye will, and it shall be done unto you" (John 15:7).** Getting answers should bring some excitement to prayer!

In order to understand the mind and will of God, it is necessary to read through entire books of the Bible, and not just jump from one section to another. A good idea is to read through a book in the Old Testament and a book in the New Testament. If you read a chapter or two from each every

---

*Solitude- there's a word you don't hear much in this day of constant media noise and social networking!

day, you would get through the entire Bible in about a year and a half. This doesn't mean you shouldn't read certain isolated sections once in a while or as God leads, but your fundamental reading should be consistent and contextual.

This will be a firm foundation, and a solid rock from which to build prayer and be transformed. It will be life changing, because God's word converts the soul, causes rejoicing, and brings wisdom and enlightenment (see **Psalm 19:7-8**).

The more familiar you get with God's Word, the easier prayer becomes. You can use what you have just read to help provide content for prayers. You can bolster your faith with the knowledge of God's works and faithfulness. You can be stirred to praise with the understanding of His love. And there are thousands of promises in the Bible that can bring strength and victory in troubling times.

Come to God with words of worship. "But I don't know what to say!" Learn this language from His very Word. Get acquainted with the worship and praises in the Psalms, and learn to praise Him in like manner. Reading or singing the words of a good worship song can also help bring us into a ready spirit for prayer. Sometimes the feelings may not be there, but often they come after praising God anyway! Praising God is a great way to stir up the heart. Feelings come and go. Faith takes action regardless of feelings, but the feelings often come after faith has been exercised.

"Be still, and know that I am God" **(Ps.46:10).** It's very hard for people to be still. Try not to be in a hurry. I believe this also means to be quiet. It is very natural to just ramble off everything that comes to mind and heart, and to be the only one doing the talking. God may want to say something to you.

"But God doesn't speak to me when I am quiet." You may be depending on your natural senses. You may be waiting for familiar English words to come to your mind. You would like to hear an audible voice. Some people do hear from God in these ways, but He may also be speaking in a way completely outside of natural understanding. This is not mystical, it is spiritual. Your spirit may be thriving in the stillness, but your thoughts and worries are making too much noise. Let everything be hushed by faith in His presence. Be still and you will know that He is God!

After a while of stillness, words may well up and need an outlet. Allow them to flow. It may be praise, petitions, or even a heavenly language. Stay in a spirit of faith and let it out.

Give thanks. Season all prayers with thanksgiving! Giving thanks encourages faith, and faith brings strength. One of the biggest mistakes often made in prayer is that it becomes a griping and complaining time. I used to think I needed to "pour out my heart," and I would go on and on telling God how bad everything was. Guess what? I felt worse for praying after that! If all we do is rehearse the bad, we will remain in bondage to it. Instead, look for the good side of every situation. If there doesn't seem to be any good side, we can at least thank God that this won't be a problem in heaven!

Sometimes I try to just get myself "into heaven" and away from this world (through prayer). The song says that when you fix your eyes upon Jesus, the things of this world will grow strangely dim. After that there is strength and renewal. But to just groan and mope over a laundry list of problems brings even more weariness.

There's a place for mentioning the problems. I'm just saying don't dwell on them for too long. Stop begging God for help and start claiming His promises. Go to the Word and find the Scriptures that can address your situation. Then in prayer thank God for the promise and ask Him to make it manifest in your situation.

Invite the Holy Spirit. Whenever we pray, we want the prayers to be spiritual. Sometimes the Lord lays a burden on the heart and it is a spiritual prayer from the very beginning. Other times it is necessary to wait on the Holy Spirit, and call upon Him to breathe His petitions through us. Sometimes we don't even know what we are praying, but the Spirit Himself is groaning within (**Romans 8:26**). The key here is to just be sensitive and aware that prayer is taking place.

Be sensitive. Remember that you are speaking to God! Prayer can often become a routine of speaking religious language with no real connection to God. It is easy to develop a pattern in which the words sound good but have nothing of the heart. Beware of falling into this. Watch out for vain repetitions- praying endlessly for the same thing, or repeating the same phrases over and over. Prayer is sometimes referred to as 'watching.' If we should watch what we say to other people, we should watch what we say to the Lord. This doesn't have to be a rigid rule, it just requires a little sensitivity.

Know that Jesus intercedes. This is the good news! After all has been said and done, God still accepts imperfect prayers from His children. He heard the prayers of Cornelius before Cornelius even believed in Jesus (**Acts 10**). How much more does he hear ours! It's been said that our prayers are like flowers being offered up to the Father. When we offer them up with weeds (our sins and imperfections), Jesus sorts them out! God is pleased with our prayers (**Prov.15:8**). As in every respect of the Christian life, we are covered.

In China, I have seen nervous ladies bow and kow-tow before porcelain statues. I have seen (in temples) idols larger than life, with hideous expressions and grotesque features. In Thailand, many places carry the stench of incense, and gigantic idols in Buddhist temples are found on every street corner. Offerings are made to little demon-houses in people's front yards. And how many minority people groups are there throughout the world, who are bound to village witch doctors and occultic practices? They are all caught in the unrelenting grips of fear. It is such a contrast to the freedom we have in Christ Jesus! We are blessed to serve a God who loves us, and to **serve him without fear (Luke 1:74).**

I am thankful for the privilege and opportunity to pray **to the King eternal, immortal, invisible, the only wise God... (1Tim.1:17).** He bids us to His throne of grace. He meets us with love, and has the desire to answer our prayers- **thy Father which seeth in secret shall reward thee openly.**

Unanswered Prayer

Objection: "I don't always get what I pray for! I don't see any rewards!"

Answer: It is interesting to note that other versions of the Bible do not have the word 'openly' where it talks of the Father's reward. The Greek for this was actually added in a later manuscript. This has significant implications. What is done in secret WILL be rewarded-- that is the promise of the Word. Often prayer will be rewarded openly with wonderfully visible results. This should be expected. But there will also be rewards given in the age to come. Jesus spoke of secret prayer being rewarded, as well as secret deeds, and secret fasting. In each instance He repeated that what was done in secret would be rewarded. Significantly, He follows up these promises with the exhortation to store up our treasures in heaven (**Matt.6:19-21**)! There are rewards coming forth openly as well as rewards storing up in heaven. The point is that you will see a return either now, later, or both.

Do you realize that your times of prayer are divine investments? The flesh may cry, "I prayed but nothing happened!" But faith will answer, "It ain't over yet! And it has already been rewarded in heaven."

Times of prayer on this earth can be the sweetest experiences we have in this life. The Christian should make it his or her aim to find that precious blessing of communion with God, and that daily. Just remember that all is not lost if the blessing is not immediately experienced. It may be that a greater reward has been laid up for you because you persevered in prayer when you felt nothing.

Go then to the storeroom, and pray in secret. And do not come out-- here I mean that the heart should stay in the state of prayer continually. Do not 'become a spiritual person' only when it is time to perform 'an act of religion.' No. When you come out of the room, or the church building, or the time of fellowship, try to stay in that frame of special alertness before the Lord. **Where your treasure is, there will your heart be also (Matt. 6:21).** The body comes out but the heart must stay in. This then will speak of a significant distinction from the 'religious' of the world.

9. Into the Wilderness

"OH NO!" The wife began to wriggle nervously in her seat.

"It's okay, honey," said the husband, "the map says it's at least a few more miles before we see the main road." He did his best to maintain a look of confidence. But as they drove on, it seemed they were anywhere but near their intended destination. The tension mounted.

"Is that it up ahead?" the wife asked with a gleam of hope. But that gleam quickly dissolved. As they went further and further down the road, the husband knew it was decision time. Should they keep going, or turn around?

Most of us husbands need to confess that it is often pride that keeps us from admitting we're lost and turning around. But every once in a while it turns out we made the right decision by continuing onward! There's a certain enjoyment of getting through the clouds of uncertainty and finding relief at the sight of the anticipated landmarks ahead.

As Christians we must always guard against pride, but NEVER turn around as we travel the straight and narrow path that leads to life! There may be uncertainty at times, but we have a map for the journey, the Word of God. It contains all the help needed to get us through the wilderness of this world. But faith is not just about "making it" through this world. The people of God have a kingdom mission.

When the Pilgrims first came to America, they found nothing but a wilderness. They didn't turn back, because they knew they had a mission.

Though they suffered through severe trials and hardships, they trusted God and stayed the course. And America eventually became an oasis!

The Bible promises that this world will eventually change. There will be **new heavens and a new earth, wherein dwelleth righteousness (2Peter 3:13).** That is referring to the final consummation. It is not just for the future, though. God wants to use His people to enact His kingdom in the here and now. He wants His will **done on earth as it is in heaven (Matt. 6:10).** Like the Pilgrims, we go into the wilderness in order to change it. Jesus **gave himself for us, that he might redeem us from all iniquity, and purify unto himself a peculiar people, zealous of good works (Titus 2:14).** He wants to change the world through the good works of His people.

It is true that the world often seems a hopeless place, but the Christian faith is not about holding on while the ship sinks. In fact, none of our labor in the Lord is in vain (**1Cor.15:58**). We can indeed transform this world while it waits for its "new body." It is similar to our own salvation. Real change has taken place and is taking place, but we don't receive our perfect bodies until the end.

The world offers trials and hardships around every corner, but God's people can offer comfort and relief. The key is to resist the devil's intimidation. He likes to roar a lot, but Jesus has overcome him. Don't turn around simply because the comfort seems to have gone. The Holy Spirit continues His work, even when we do not feel it. He knows how to turn the dryness and difficulties of the wilderness into refreshing fruit for those who persevere in faith.

Wilderness Experience

Through Christ, it is possible to go through this world with gospel peace and joy. However, it is very common to experience times when you really do feel like you are struggling through a wilderness.

The early American poets, Emerson and Thoreau, viewed the wilderness as a place of escape and contact with the divine. Christians, however, often find the wilderness a desolate place they want to escape. Like

Jesus experienced, it is a place of contact with temptation. It is in the wilderness that the children of Israel fell prey to unbelief and wound up as dead carcasses.

To *come out from their midst and be separate* is to leave the comforts of Egypt. When Israel came out of Egypt, they escaped their bondage, but they ended up in a wilderness. They missed all the good food they once enjoyed (see Numbers 11:5-7). They murmured and complained about that and other problems, and eventually found defeat. Only those who were faithful experienced the later blessings.

By contrast, John the Baptist lived in the wilderness by choice. For him, the wilderness was not a bad place at all. It kept him safe from the false and hypocritical teachers of the day. It provided an atmosphere for him to grow strong in the Spirit (**Luke 1:80**). He was able to look to the coming Christ without the distractions of the material world. This is not to say he cut himself off completely. He didn't become a cloistered monk. At the appointed time, he had contact with the multitudes and fulfilled the work that had been given to him. The wilderness, though certainly not comfortable, was an instrument of divine anointing. And when all was said and done, Jesus testified, **"among them that are born of women there hath not risen a greater than John the Baptist" (Matt.11:11).**

John the Baptist can be viewed as a type (symbolic) of the church. It is the church's great work to prepare the way of the Lord. As John looked to His first coming, the church looks to His second coming. The church also preaches repentance unto salvation, and baptizes the nations with water. The difference, though, is that the church is not born of women but of the Spirit. In this sense the church is greater.

The Lord used John's time in the wilderness to work up authority and power in his life. No one likes to be in a wilderness time, but it is likely that such seasons in our lives are used by God to build us up for the works ahead. Moses had his time in the wilderness before God called him to speak before Pharaoh. Elijah had his time with the ravens before his major ministry came to fruition. Jesus Himself spent time in the wilderness before appearing publicly.

A lot could be learned from Jesus' trial in the desert (see Luke 4:1-13). It should at least be clear that a great spiritual victory had occurred. We can look at the first man, Adam, who had *everything* in the land of Paradise, and lost it all to the devil in the first round. Here we have the 'last Adam,' Jesus Christ, who had *nothing* in the middle of the desert. Physically famished and weak, the devil could get nothing from Him! After several rounds, the devil had to retreat until a more opportune time. Jesus had reclaimed for man what Adam had lost.

Jesus received an anointing at His baptism, but the wilderness seemed to perfect it. From there He went on into His ministry with sanctified power. **Though he were a Son, yet learned he obedience by the things which he suffered; and being made perfect, he became the author of eternal salvation unto all them that obey him (Heb.5:8-9).**

Joy in the Wilderness

The wilderness is a time of waiting on the Lord. It is a time to dig into the Word and exercise faith and trust. It is not to be feared, but as James said,

> **My brethren, count it all joy when you fall into various trials; knowing this, that the testing of your faith produces patience. But let patience have its perfect work, that you may be perfect and complete, lacking nothing. (James 1:2-4; NKJV).**

So many believers want to go into ministry with an anointing, but they do not want to go through the necessary pains of having that anointing perfected. I remember the old comic book advertisements that used to show a huge muscle-man flexing his biceps and the headline blurted out, "YOU CAN LOOK LIKE THIS IN JUST 10 DAYS!!!" They might be able to fool an immature child, but anyone with a little wisdom knows that such a hulking figure requires more than that, and there is no easy way to become as big as Arnold!

Trials are not easy, but one way to a hulking spirituality is to consider it joyful that you have a faith that is adequate for your various trials. This doesn't mean you should invite trials or see them as God trying to teach you something. God is not the one doing the tempting (**James 1:13**). But your faith will grow and learn as the trials drive you to the Word, and you search out help from any Scriptures that apply to your situation. You will also grow stronger as you learn how to resist the devil. That's the way weightlifters get stronger—through resistance. They persevere through the workouts because they have an eye on the good that will result. According to James, trials should be viewed in the same way.

That is not to say that it's wrong to groan under trials. There is a groaning that can be positive. Weight lifters will groan and grunt as they pump their iron, but it is with a determination and desire. They have their goals in sight, and know how the pressure of the weights works to fulfill them. They even invite greater hardship by adding more weights to their workout. We do not need to invite greater hardships, but we can learn from their example.

If they have been consistent, they will find themselves getting stronger. What once seemed heavy will become manageable. It can bring joy to realize that trials can produce the same effect (spiritually). It is a blessing to really understand that they can be turned around for something good in our lives.

God's love is not just in the immediate sense of His presence. It's good to always seek His immediate presence. But those who believe can also find God's love even through the hardships. The extra weights that are thrown upon the soul cannot stop the love of God, and it is up to us to believe that in spite of the difficult times we might be in.

Such times always come to pass! They seem they will go on forever, but they don't. The Lord gets us through it all. Then we in turn can go out into the world and help others. Because we received His comfort in our trial, we are better equipped to comfort others (**2Cor. 1:4**). That is one way of changing the world.

The world is a desperate wilderness, but God's people are the hope of this world. They are not exempt from the troubles, but they know where true help comes from. Then as ambassadors of the kingdom, they offer it to those who are needy.

To come out and be separate, be ready. Don't be afraid of the mission field (and by the mission field I mean everywhere, at home or abroad!). The world is the valley of the shadow of death, but **though I walk through the valley of the shadow of death, I will fear no evil: for thou art with me (Ps.23:4).** Ministry will provide many opportunities for discouragement because it takes place in the wilderness. Resist discouragement, persevere, and you will see God come through in great ways.

A Word About Patience

Early on in our China ministry, my wife and I helped at an orphanage every week. Some missionaries started to come as well, but did not continue. It wasn't easy and it was often depressing. However, after about a year we began to see wonderful things happen. Some of the greatest blessings occurred, and we could have missed them if we hadn't plodded through the rough times before.

> **Be patient therefore, brethren, unto the coming of the Lord. Behold, the husbandman waiteth for the precious fruit of the earth, and hath long patience for it, until he receive the early and latter rain. Be ye also patient; establish your hearts: for the coming of the Lord draweth nigh. (James 5:7-8).**

Keep the end in sight. Never forget the coming of the Lord. A vision of this puts all suffering and waiting into perspective. For the love of Rachel, Jacob worked seven years and they seemed to him but a few days (**Gen.29:20**). At the coming of the Lord all time passed will seem as nothing. It helps to get a vision for this.

Consider also, that the coming of the Lord is *at hand.* It is nearer than we know! This applies not just to the actual return of Jesus, but also to the blessing that comes upon our work for Him. Does your ministry seem fruitless? It requires the coming of the Lord into the work. Behold, the farmer waits for the precious fruit of the earth. The early and latter rains are the necessary preparation for the crops. God uses events past and present to accomplish the overall scope of His work. Know that He is working. It may be the season of early rain, and He is accomplishing through you some preliminary foundations. Or, it may be the season of latter rain, and the harvest is soon to be reaped.

We may enjoy the reaping now, or it may be reserved for later, or even in the age to come. Whenever it is, it will be precious fruit. **Wait on the LORD: be of good courage, and he shall strengthen thine heart: wait, I say, on the LORD (Ps.27:14).**

10. The Results of Coming Out

> **Then shall we know, if we follow on to know the LORD: his going forth is prepared as the morning; and he shall come unto us as the rain, as the latter and former rain unto the earth (Hosea 6:3).**

HAVE YOU EVER tried to follow somebody in a car? Most of us have had the experience of trying to keep up with someone ahead of us. It is not a very difficult task on an empty road, but get out on a crowded highway and it requires a lot more concentration.

The word is, **then shall we know, if we follow on to know the LORD...** We will have this intimate inner knowledge of the divine if we follow Him. Like following in a car, we have to keep Him in sight. It is not very difficult as we travel down Spiritual Street or Communion Court, but if we are not careful, we might lose Him on Distraction Drive. As we merge onto the Highway of Life, many other vehicles can easily get between us, so it is important to stay focused.

Staying focused, *then shall we know...* "We already know this," one says. Again, this is different from simply believing and having head knowledge. Then shall we KNOW. The Hebrew for this word (yada) entails a depth of knowing in an intimate way. It is more than just knowing, it is a perceiving, a recognizing, an experiencing, a skillful understanding, and more. *Then shall we know...* The best way to describe it might be the answer we give to someone when we can't really explain it: *"I just know."*

The followers will find great joy and strength in *knowing* that his going forth is prepared as the morning. This means it's a certainty. The good news is that **the night is far spent, the day is at hand (Rom.13:12).** There is a great resurrection coming, and God will have His work accomplished in His saints. He shall come unto us as the rain, as the latter and former rain unto the earth. There shall be showers of blessing! He will be our God, and we shall be His people, and His victory will be exalted throughout the earth.

Victory in Jesus!

This is not just a prophetic word for the future, it is for here and now as well. The physical consummation of the victory of Jesus and His people is a sure event to be anticipated. But it also speaks of the spiritual victory that is available now to His followers. In the darkest of nights, He can shine like the bright Morning Star. In our driest of times, He can water us with the latter and former rains. In the loneliest circumstances, we can find Him coming unto us. He is already with us. He has promised to never leave us nor forsake us (**Heb.13:5**)! We have to come out and be separate from the unbelief that causes us to think He doesn't care. We have to separate from what our feelings or circumstances might be telling us. What is the truth according to God's Word? That is where the reality is, and faith will overcome by receiving the truth and rejecting the lies. **Let God be true, but every man a liar (Rom. 3:4).**

We become partakers of His divine nature through **His exceeding great and precious promises (2Peter 1:4).** The problem is that many Christians don't look for the words of life that will sustain them in their particular trials. They may, for example, worry themselves into sickness over their financial situation, when they could instead cling to the promise that **my God shall supply all your need according to his riches in glory by Christ Jesus (Philippians 4:19).** They may allow life to overwhelm them with a seemingly impossible situation, but **all things are possible to him that believeth (Mark 9:23).**

The Lord will often manifest His presence in special ways to help carry us through. When the Lord reveals Himself to us in these wonderful ways, we become more equipped to meet others and to be a blessing. We are more apt to bring change to our environment (which is something America desperately needs). And we no longer fear death. We find it is the key that brings in resurrection glory, now and beyond.

His revelation can come in extraordinary ways, and should be hoped for and expected. But this way is like icing on the cake. Believers already have the revelation they need in the promises of God, and the strength and grace is available immediately upon simply believing His Word for the situation. There is power in the Word!

There is power in the Spirit. The Bible says that believers have been sealed with the Holy Spirit (**Eph.4:30**). If you have not received the Holy Spirit, ask and He shall be given (**Luke 11:13**). Peter said that **the promise is unto you, and to your children, and to all that are afar off, even as many as the Lord our God shall call (Acts 2:39).** It is because Jesus shed His blood for us that we can receive from Him the greatest Gift.

There is power in the blood! **How much more shall the blood of Christ, who through the eternal Spirit offered himself without spot to God, purge your conscience from dead works to serve the living God? (Heb. 9:14).** The blood has made a way for us to be free from any guilt. It cleanses us, and no matter what spots or blemishes are found in our works, they are acceptable to God through the blood. The blood brings liberty to those who are bogged down and accused by a tender conscience. Because of the blood, God is not mad at us. As Andrew Wommack says, "He's not even in a bad mood!"

So we have the power of the Word, the Spirit, and the Blood. On top of that is the love of the Father and His care for us. We have so much power that Jesus said, **"Verily, verily, I say unto you, He that believeth on me, the works that I do shall he do also; and greater works than these shall he do; because I go unto my Father" (John 14:12).** One reason so little power is seen in the church is because so few people believe that they really have it. The unbelief and materialism of the world tend to dominate even people of faith. In many circles, religious tradition and legalism add to the problem. Many in the body of Christ have become ensnared by denominationalism and "safe" religious atmospheres guided more by systematic theology and philosophies of worship than by childlike readiness for world-changing and life-changing moves of God.

The apostle Paul said, **"I can do all things through Christ which strengtheneth me" (Phil.4:13).** And he did, as he endured beatings, hunger, nakedness, and trials of all sorts for the sake of Jesus. Some church members can't even endure a change in the color of paint on the walls, or the order of a service!

Paul could have played it safe and preached a traditional Jewish message, only incorporating Jesus into it to some degree. Instead, Jesus replaced the entire Jewish message. It was all about Him. The cherished law was no longer the focus. Paul brought a lot of trouble to himself, but it didn't seem to faze him. He went on in supernatural power and got supernatural results. We wouldn't even remember him or be discussing him if he simply played it safe. He came out and separated himself from the status quo religion and embarked on an incredible journey of faith. It was faith in a God who loved him, a former persecutor. It was faith in the work of Jesus instead of adherence to religious traditions and rules. The result was freedom and world-changing power. On the other hand, the sticklers to tradition are all but forgotten.

Persecution Inevitable

The devil does not take lightly to those who would excel in the faith. **Yea, and all that will live godly in Christ Jesus shall suffer persecution (2Tim.3:12).** If it is not physical, it will be spiritual persecution from the principalities and powers that surround us.

I think we brush this off too lightly however. We should probably be experiencing (at some point or other) actual persecution from man. Living according to a higher standard should indeed make somebody uncomfortable around us. There are times of favor, but history shows time and time again that great moves of God are met by opposition.

There is a story about John Wesley, who we love as a great evangelist but who was also a great influence in the history of England. At a certain time in his ministry he found himself constantly the target of persecution from corrupt churchmen and 'high society' officials. He had brushes with mobs. But he accepted all this as confirmation that he was in the right place of obedience to God. We must be doing something right if the enemy is worried enough to bring on so many attacks.

At a certain time, however, he encountered a few days in which he suffered no attacks whatsoever. This did not bring relief, but worry! Outside he prayed, asking the Lord if he had done anything wrong. Somebody at that time saw him and threw a brick at him. For this, he thanked God and praised Him that things were still okay!

Wesley KNEW. Paul KNEW. May we all KNOW. It is enough to make us forsake all for Jesus. It is time for the church (all of us) to come out. It is time to leave house, family, lands, --all for the sake of Jesus. Whether this is literal or not, it must happen within our hearts. We have a high calling to answer, but we have a High Priest to help us. And this great High Priest has promised:

> **"Verily I say unto you, There is no man that hath left house, or brethren, or sisters, or father, or mother, or wife, or children, or lands, for my sake, and the gospel's, But he shall receive an hundredfold now in this time, houses, and brethren, and sisters, and mothers, and children, and lands, with persecutions; and in the world to come eternal life." (Mark 10:29-30).**

In the world to come, eternal life! Did you hear that? Eternal life! It even begins in the here and know by knowing Jesus (**John 17:3**). The world can only offer death. The choice should be simple. The path of faith may not always be easy, but it will be more than worth it.

Make the decision not to turn back. Be ready for that temptation, and then follow the example of the Christian in *Pilgrim's Progress*: "he had not run far from his own door, but his wife and children perceiving it began to cry after him to return; but the man put his fingers in his ears and ran on crying, Life! Life! Eternal life!"

Let's help each other along the way, and in the end we will meet together around the throne of the most Worthy Lamb and enjoy His unhindered presence forever and ever. We will have come out from the midst of corruption and trouble, and have entered into glory and bliss.

Separation will no longer be a necessity. The Kingdom of Heaven will cover the earth and God will be all in all (**1Corinthians 15:28**).

AMEN.

Study Guide

Suggestions:

- To start discussion, ask if anything stood out or made an impression in the chapter.

- Where several verses are listed, (in a group setting) divide them up for different individuals to read.

- If a discussion starts to take off, don't feel bound to the questions. Let there be a free flow…

- On the other hand, if a discussion is going off on a tangent, or a point is being over emphasized, don't be afraid to pull everyone back on track.

- Ask God to give revelation and understanding.

Chapter 1
Who Needs to Come Out?

1. What are true riches? Name examples of true riches in Christ and how they excel the world's riches. Then compare your answers with these: John 10:10; John 14:16-17, 27; John 17:22; Romans 8:18, 37-39; Colossians 1:27; 1Corinthians 1:30; 2Corinthians 8:9, 9:8; Philippians 4:13, 19. Rev.21:4. (Not an exhaustive list).

2. Why is it sometimes difficult to enjoy these riches and/or share them with others? Possible answers may include Matthew 17:20; 1Peter 5:6-9; Romans 1:21.

3. Read Luke 9:51-56. Why did Jesus rebuke the disciples? Discuss how the presence of Jesus should look in our lives, in contrast to strict religious activity.

4. The students pushed and shoved to get on the bus. In contrast, give a testimony of someone who really impressed you with a godly action or response in a particular situation.

5. Jesus spoke of asking for the Spirit (Luke 11:13), receiving the Spirit (John 20:22), and being empowered by the Spirit (Acts 1:8). Besides being born again, have you asked for and received this filling and empowering? What does it result in? Galatians 5:16-26. 1Corinthians 12:31; 14:1.

6. How is receiving God's love different from believing God's love? Ephesians 3:16-19; John 14:21; 1John 4:16.

7. How do you keep yourself in God's love? Jude 21.

8. You find out that your "friend" has told a lie about you. Would you: a. tell a lie about your friend? b. stop being friends? c. try to defend yourself? d. get even in some other way? e: other:_____?

9. What does the Word teach us about doing good when we are wronged? 1Peter 3:9-12, 4:13-14; Romans 12:17-21.

10. In what way was Jesus a 'separated' Man? Give examples of what made Him or makes Him unique among men. Christian separation can be attractive like that of Jesus, or unattractive like that of the Pharisees. Note the differences.

Chapter 2
Why We Must Come Out

1. How would you differentiate "mainstream Christianity" from Biblical faith? Give examples.

2. Read 1Timothy 6:3-5 and 20-21. What "faulty perception" of faith is Paul dealing with here and what should faith be involved with instead?

3. Have you lived by any faulty perceptions of the faith? How did you change?

4. Read Romans 12:2 and 1Peter 2:1-3. How does transformation take place in the Christian life?

5. Read Psalm 1:2-3. Concerning transformation or growth, what kind of effort is involved here? How have you usually tried to make progress?

6. Is it possible to meditate on the Word day and night? (Consider that worry is a negative form of meditation. That is easy enough to keep in our thoughts even while occupied with other things.) See 2Corinthians 10:5.

7. Discuss how God's best is for now and not just the future. See 1Timothy 4:8; 1John 4:17, and 3John 2

8. Your workmates or classmates begin gossiping about a very annoying person. You also find the person annoying. How do you respond?

9. "Biblical separation means living differently." What are some ways that you can start living differently in order to reflect God's love in the world?

10. If we do not earn heaven by works, why is it important that we be holy?

Chapter 3
How to Come Out and Be Separate

1. Share a testimony of a time or situation that God brought you to your 'spiritual senses' and you came out.

2. Read Titus 2:11-14. What teaches us to live holy? How is holiness usually preached?

3. According to the above passage, what is the vision needed that will propel us?

4. Discuss what might have made the prodigal son zealous to do good, and tie it to the Titus passage above.

5. What is vision? How can one get a vision?

6. Read Ephesians 1:17-20. Paul is praying for vision concerning several things. What are they? Discuss what you already understand about them.

7. Discuss the importance of words. Are words valued or thought out much today? Proverbs 10:19; 13:2-3; 21:23; Psalm 19:14.

8. James 2:17 says that faith without works is dead. How might the story of the prodigal son be used to illustrate this point?

9. How does thankfulness keep our hearts softened towards God? Romans 1:21.

10. Do you have any other ideas about how to come out and be separate (that weren't mentioned)?

[Remember, steer clear of legalism!]

Chapter 4
Coming Out in Fellowship

1. Share with each other your favorite book of the Bible and/or favorite verse, and why.

2. Do you find it easier to share like this in a Bible study setting than over lunch with a friend? Why?

3. Read Acts 4:32. What hinders Christians from being like this today?

4. Discuss the relationship between the heart and fellowship. Matthew 12:34-35; 15:18; Proverbs 4:20-23.

5. Besides encouragement, what else happens in fellowship? Hebrews 10:24; Matthew 18:20; Romans 1:11-12; Colossians 2:2; 1John 1:3-4.

6. Do you agree that entertainment can become a god? Does entertainment influence the ways of our culture or do the ways of our culture influence entertainment?

7. Read Psalm 19:1-4. How do the heavens speak of God? Can God enter into any subject we talk about?

8. Read John 4: 7-14. How did Jesus initiate and maintain the spiritual conversation?

9. What are some good ways to start a spiritual conversation?

10. I'm the kind of person who:
 a. likes to be around lots of people   b. prefers one to one interaction
 c. would rather stay home and_____   d. other?

Chapter 5
Coming Out with Joy

1. Besides your relationship with God, what brings you the most joy in life?

2. Does the Lord care about our happiness or is He more concerned with our holiness? John 15:11; 17:13; Philippians 4:4; Hebrews 3:6; Romans 14:17.

3. Should one expect to struggle in trying to live a godly life? Matthew 11:30; 2Timothy 3:12.

4. Jesus was described as a "Man of sorrows" (Isaiah 53:3). How was He a Man of sorrows? Discuss how that works along with Luke 10:21; Hebrews 1:9; 12:2.

5. If you are not experiencing joy and peace, does it necessarily mean that you are not believing?

6. How can someone stir up their faith? Romans 12:2; Ephesians 4:22-24; James 4:7-8.

7. "I have faith in Jesus," says Slim. He can quote all kinds of Scripture and argue over theology, but he tells dirty jokes at work and complains that he can't control his anger. What elements of faith does he seem to be missing? How would you advise him if he were willing to listen?

8. Read Zephaniah 3:13-20. List the different promises in this passage that should encourage hope and joy.

9. Of those different promises, which ones are just as true for now as well as in the future?

10. Read 2 Corinthians 8:9. In what ways are we rich? How should thinking about this affect our walk?

Chapter 6
Coming Out to Serve

1. Have you ever had a time that you were serving and doing something difficult, yet you enjoyed it? Share one instance.

2. Read Romans 12:1. What does it mean to present your body as a living sacrifice? Discuss, and then compare your answer with Exodus 21:1-6.

3. Read Psalm 100. What thoughts expressed in this Psalm would help encourage joyful service to God?

4. Explain how vision is needed for serving God. Besides your answers, check Matthew 25:21; 1Corinthians 3:12-14; Matthew 6:10; and 1Corinthians 15:58.

5. If you are stuck in an unpleasant work situation, what can you think upon in order to help change your attitude? Besides your answers, check Ephesians 6:5-8; 1Peter 1:3-7, 5:6-7; and Philippians 4:6-9.

6. What is the proper motive in giving?

7. Many Christians are seeking to know God's will. How does one learn what God's will is? Besides your answers, check Romans 12:2; Psalm 119:101-105; and Habakkuk 2:1-4.

8. Can you share an experience where you found and knew God's will for something?

9. Read Acts 6:1-6. What were the qualifications for those who would serve tables? How do we look at such service today?

10. Are there any new ways that you and your group can think of to serve one another or to serve as a team?

Chapter 7
Coming Out of a Rut

1. Start this discussion differently than you normally do. Have each person think of a line from a favorite Christian song or hymn and say it, while the others guess what song or hymn it is. Or do some exercises, like sit-ups or push-ups. [It doesn't matter, just do something different!]

2. Read Romans 7:6. According to this verse, what may be some causes of getting stuck in a rut?

3. Read Colossians 3:9-17. Is newness something that just happens to you? What is your role according to these verses?

4. What advice would you give to someone who says, "I try to read the Bible but I just find it boring."?

5. What book or books have you read that really inspired your faith? (If no books, song, film, other?)

6. Read 2Samuel 6:12-22. What lessons about worship can be learned from this passage?

7. What is Jesus' advice to the church in the rut, per Revelation 2:4-5 and 3:18-21?

8. Read Acts 4:29-31. Was this a dull prayer meeting? How does it differ from a typical prayer meeting today? What were their expectations? Do you expect Acts type of miracles?

9. Read Galatians 5:25 and Romans 8:5. What is the difference between living in the Spirit and walking in the Spirit?

10. Some people have a hard time enjoying prayer. How might you try something new in the way you pray?

Chapter 8
One Place NOT to Come Out Of

1. Why is it important to spend time in prayer?

2. Share a testimony of answered prayer.

3. Discuss what you think a proper balance between mentioning problems, making requests, and praising God in prayer should be.

4. How did Jesus and the apostles pray for healing? Matthew 8:3; 9:6; Mark 9:25; Luke 4:39; Acts 3:6; 9:34, 40; 14:9-20; 28:8.

5. Read Mark 6:46 and Luke 6:12. Discuss how you think Jesus might have spent His prayer time.

6. What are the benefits of having a daily quiet time?

7. Discuss how reading the Bible can be a part of prayer times and help fuel prayer.

8. Examine some prayers of Paul in Colossians 4:12; Romans 15:30-32; Ephesians 1:16-19; 3:16-19; 6:19; Philippians 1:9-11; 1 Thessalonians 5:25; and 2Thessalonians 3:1. What makes up the content of his prayers? What makes up the content of most of our prayers?

9. Read 1Thessalonians 5:17-18. We obviously cannot sit and have a quiet time without ceasing. What do you think Paul means here?

10. Philippians 4:19 says, "my God shall supply all your needs..." This is a promise that can be used often in prayer. Can you think of other good promises to use in prayer for different situations?

Chapter 9
Into the Wilderness

1. When you have lost your way, are you quick to stop and ask directions or would you rather just keep going?

2. If we are saved through faith, what role do good works play in the Christian life? Ephesians 2:10; Titus 2:14; 2Timothy 3:17; Hebrews 10:24; 1Peter 2:12.

3. How can viewing the world as "a wilderness" help you cope in a hopeless situation?

4. Hebrews 11:13-14 speaks of the faithful as "strangers and pilgrims on earth" seeking a better homeland. Do you think this characterizes the church in our day? In what ways are we too at home here? In what ways are we excelling?

5. What are some similarities between John the Baptist and the church? What are some differences?

6. This chapter briefly contrasted Jesus' wilderness victory with Adam's paradise fall. Expand on this using Romans 5:14-19.

7. How can our wilderness victories become blessings to others?

8. Discuss how these verses might help us deal with trials: Matthew 11:28-30; Acts 14:22; and John 16:33.

9. Does suffering mean that you are not blessed? Ephesians 1:3; Galatians 6:9.

10. Discuss the role of patience in the walk of faith, and the different ways that God is patient.

Chapter 10
The Results of Coming Out

1. Discuss the results of religion vs. the results of relationship (with God). What are the similarities and differences?

2. What does it mean to follow Jesus? Where is He leading us?

3. What is eternal life, according to John 17:3? When does this happen? John 10:10.

4. When is eternal life, according to Mark 10:30? How can we harmonize this with the answer to question 3?

5. What are the works that we can expect to do, alluded to in John 14:12?

6. Paul came out from the "status quo" of the Jewish religion and got in trouble. According to Galatians 5:11, what was the offense of the cross? Does the cross offend today in the same manner?

7. Read 1Thessalonians 1:5-10. What were the results of the Thessalonians' faithfulness?

8. What is it that brings on persecution according to 2Timothy 3:12? Is that the only thing that brings it on? What else? Can you think of any examples/reasons Christians might bring on persecution needlessly?

9. Sometimes we do not need results but have to believe they have already been accomplished. Read Colossians 3:1-4. What has already happened and what is yet to happen?

10. You have now come out and become separate! What is the next step? Where do we go from here?

You Might also Enjoy

Win Christ

Having faith means more than holding traditions, morals and values. *Win Christ* presents a model for grace, victory and power in the spiritual life. The Biblical truths combined with personal experiences and historic anecdotes will inspire and encourage readers both young and old.

Includes a Group Discussion and Bible Study guide.

The One Who Overcomes: Perseverance and Victory in the Book of Revelation

Passing by the speculations and concentrating more on the spiritual truths behind the prophecy, *The One Who Overcomes* presents the book of Revelation in an easy to understand and practical manner.

This is *not* an analysis of how current events line up with Biblical prophecy. Instead, it is a look at Revelation in terms of what the believer can use *now* in his or her spiritual journey.

These books are available through:
www.ricksbell.com